THE MONEY DECEPTION

*What Banks & Governments
Don't Want You to Know*

Distribution of the securities market key players

the activity of the
passive market is
Established positive
arious market seg-

12%

BGY

FEW

RDW

THOMAS HEROLD

THE MONEY DECEPTION

What Banks and Governments Don't Want You to Know

Revision 2.01

Thomas Herold

moneydeception.com

Table of Contents

Copyright & Disclaimer

What is Deception?

From the Merriam Webster Dictionary

1. a) The act of causing someone to accept as true or valid what is false or invalid : the act of deceiving resorting to falsehood and deception used deception to leak the classified information

    b) the fact or condition of being deceived the deception of his audience

2. Something that deceives : trick fooled by a scam artist's clever deception

Synonyms from Thesaurus.com

beguilement, betrayal, blarney, boondoggle, *cheat*, circumvention, cozenage, craftiness, cunning, deceit, deceitfulness, deceptiveness, defraudation, dirt, *disinformation*, dissimulation, double-dealing, dupery, duplicity, equivocation, *falsehood*, fast one, flim-flam, *fraud*, fraudulence, guile, hokum, hypocrisy, imposition, insincerity, juggling, legerdemain, *lying*, mendacity, pretense, prevarication, sophism, treachery, treason, trickery, trickiness, trumpery, *untruth* (cursive highlighted words by author).

From Wikipedia

Deception is the act of propagating beliefs in things that are not true, or not the whole truth (as in half-truths or omission). Deception can involve dissimulation, propaganda, and sleight of hand, as well as distraction, camouflage, or concealment.

Deception is a major relational transgression that often leads to feelings of betrayal and distrust between relational partners. Deception violates relational rules and is considered to be a negative violation of expectations. Most people expect friends, relational partners, and even strangers to be truthful most of the time. If people expected most conversations to be untruthful, talking and communicating with others would require distraction and misdirection to acquire reliable information. A significant amount of deception occurs between some romantic and relational partners.

Deception includes several types of communications or omissions that serve to distort or omit the complete truth. Examples of deception range from false statements to misleading claims in which relevant information is omitted, leading the receiver to infer false conclusions.

Introduction

"Let me issue and control a nation's money and I care not who writes the laws." - Mayer Amschel Rothschild, Banker and the founder of the Rothschild banking dynasty

You would think, that with the trillions of dollars the banks have unleashed since 2008 by the simple act of pressing a few keystrokes on their computers, we would bath in abundance. Sadly to say, just the opposite has happened.

Rents and housing prices are skyrocketing. Health care costs rise astronomical and obesity still increases. Most major necessities like cars and housing are only affordable through governments intervention. Even two incomes from couples are no longer enough to survive. We have more conveniences, but less time. We have more degrees but less sense; more knowledge but less judgment; more experts, but more problems; more medicines but less healthiness.

What has happened to the promise of the industrial revolution to free us from all the burden of heavy work? With all the technological advancements we have achieved - you would think - we enjoy abundance in our life. Unfortunately, in our current monetary system, the majority of technology serves money and profit instead of people. This means that sustainability and abundance will never occur in a profit system, as it goes against the fundamental idea of the structure.

Therefore, it is impossible to have a world without war, or poverty. It is impossible to advance technology to its most efficient and productive states continually. Most dramatically, it is impossible to expect human beings to behave in genuinely ethical or decent ways. [1]

Efficiency, sustainability, and abundance are the enemies of profit. It is the mechanism of scarcity that increases profits.

Do you feel like something is desperately wrong with the system but can't place your finger on it? Your current approach to protecting and growing your money and maybe even making money in the so-called ‚New Economy' is broken and not performing like it once did.

You've trusted your golden years to Wall Street, and now you're mad at the misguidance and clear negligence that has taken place. Your expenses are eating you alive. You're realizing that what used to be a healthy, respectable living making at least $75.000 to $100.000 per year is now suddenly low-level income. You're angry that you can't afford to do all the things you want to do in life, often realizing that there is more month at the end of the money.

Inequality is now higher than it has been at any time in the last century. The gaps in wages, income, and wealth are more extensive than they are in any other democratic and developed economy. On each of these fronts, inequality has grown more in the United States than it has elsewhere.

Wealth disparity in the United States is running twice as wide as wealth gaps in the rest of the industrial world. The middle class in the United States has less than half the wealth share of middle classes in much of the rest of the developed world.

The incomes of the poorest 10% of people increased by less than $3 a year between 1988 and 2011, while salaries of the wealthiest 1% grew 182 times as much. Eighty-two percent of the wealth generated last year went to the wealthiest one percent of the global population, while the 3.7 billion people who make up the most miserable half of the world saw no increase in their wealth. Billionaire wealth has risen by an annual average of 13 percent since 2010 – six times faster than the wages of ordinary workers, which have increased by a yearly average of just 2 percent.[2]

By now 1% of the population control 50% of all wealth!

False and dangerously misleading Wall Street and government statistics you see in the news have been designed to hoodwink the public and apply malicious economic rebirth and false job growth. Wall Streeters give different advice to their clients than they provide their own families. While you sleep at night, while you go to work each day, something insidious is stealing your financial future.

What I am about to unveil to you will challenge everything you've ever been taught about making money, financial planning and wealth. The facts you will read may be shocking, shameful, and to anyone who cares about their hard-earned money and the financial future of their children, outright disturbing. These facts may even upset you. They will make you uncomfortable. You may well be tempted to reject them instantly. It's natural for you to want to move away from anything causing you discomfort; however, a great deal of growth and success is preceded by pain, trouble or challenge.

You will come to understand why what's happening in the economy is intentionally not being reported on the evening news; how the same mistakes of the Great Depression are being repeated right now. Why the most significant risk in the years ahead is financially uneducated and how the financial services industry is cleverly exploiting those who are uneducated and ignorant about money.

According to the World Bank as of the start of the new decade, 28 percent are living paycheck to paycheck, 23 percent over age 65 live in poverty. Nearly 80 percent of those that reached retirement age say they cannot afford to retire. There are reasons why this is happening. As always, the unprepared and uneducated will suffer the most as they keep their savings and investments in banks and assets, which will lose the most to an evil force that most have no clue about currency inflation. Like it or not, there are secret laws, hidden forces that are now in place.

Inside this book, you will learn why the Fed (Federal Reserve System) was created and why you and I have been kept in the dark about it. You will find out why the US dollar is quietly being destroyed and the reason you and me are being led to believe otherwise. You will see why the unemployment numbers along with many other economic figures are rigged and how you and I are being lied to about it.

Albert Einstein once said: „The definition of insanity is doing the same things over and over again and expecting different results." If you keep doing what you've always done in the past when it comes to protecting and growing your money and creating cash flow, how will things change for you in the future? The most significant transfer of wealth in history is unfolding behind your back.

The next financial crisis that is already looming will be much more significant than what you saw in 2008. The crisis beyond the crisis is quietly underway. You will only become a victim of it if you continue to be uninformed and do nothing. This book will help you with significant and crucial information, but eventually, you have to act on it as well.

If money is created out of thin air, how is it possible that there is never enough of it?

The financial complexity that has been added over the last 20-30 years ensures even more profit for the banks. The money schemas are now so complicated that you need an army of financial lawyers and mathematicians to sieve through stacks of paper and complex formulas to understand how money is created merely out of thin air.

The current monetary system is designed to create winners and losers. The biggest losers in this game were in the past the Third World countries, as they have been seduced into opening their financial markets to currency manipulation. They have become helpless to the IMF (International Monetary Fund) or World Bank, as they lost their ability to control their currency. Meanwhile, they are all forced to run ever increasing amounts of debt and struggle more than ever before.

By now the financial system has hit a home run and the economic system is dangerously close to collapse - again. Did you know that in 2008 the United States was 3 hours short before declaring national bankrupt?

This whole gigantic financial system is like a big balloon - way too much air for its thin size and therefore close to exploding, and its numerous patches provide it from deflating.

This book will teach you the foundation and principles of money and the modern monetary system. It was written with the intent to give you a solid understanding, where the money comes from, how money works, and the legal methods banks and governments use it to steal your wealth. But what good will this information be if you don't know what you can do about it? Therefore, in part two you will also learn the ideas and principles to free yourself from being trapped in this toxic ,money system' and use it to create wealth for yourself and others.

You will also gain profound insight why the current monetary system is a massive patchwork of fixes and holes, and why it will come to an end very soon. Last time the financial system completely changed was in August 1971 as Nixon abandoned the gold standard. I anticipate the start of significant global changes as early as autumn 2018.

The first few chapters will give you an overview of the most powerful system in the world. It will explain in simplified terms how it got into place, and how it has now dominated and enslaved the whole planet. You will also come to realize, that at the moment, the majority of people understand how it works, the entire construct will collapse.

Reading these first few paragraphs may make you feel scary and shocked, but it is necessary to understand which principles we all operate our daily lives. It is urgent today to start making conscious decisions, which are in alignment with long-term goals to live sustainable with our planet. It is our planet - and probably the only one for a long time - from where we get our resources.

I remember the time - after digging through dozens of financial books - when one morning the whole economic puzzle revealed itself to me. There it was finally, hidden before in fractions of pieces of encrypted lingo, a clear and simple picture of how money is running the entire planet. For several days my mind felt paralyzed about the topic of money. I didn't know how to deal with cash anymore - almost like a system crash on a computer. After a reboot - it took me another five years to understand the only possible solutions, which I will reveal to you in part three of this book.

If you think the financial meltdown, which started in 2008 is fixed, I must disappoint you. In 2008 you just saw the tip of the iceberg. My intention is not to scare you or get you panicking, nor to join any conspiracy theories. All information in this book is based on facts and evidence that is available to you, but not necessarily easy to find and comprehend.

My purpose is to illustrate to you, that these dramatic changes are necessary for us as a human species to evolve further. The old monetary system will transform into a new one, which will give us more freedom to create wealth for everybody and not just for the 1-2%.

You will learn that real wealth has nothing to do with money at all! I will explain in detail why so many of us have been fallen into the trap of thinking that money is wealth. The realization that money has nothing to do with wealth will profoundly free yourself from the pressure of going after money. It will feel as if someone has taken the burden away from you, and for the first time, you can breathe freely and deeply.

In the last few chapters, I will describe what possible solution could replace the monetary system. I will compare the old system with the new system and show you how much more advantage we will gain from it. The moment you realize how restricted our current monetary policy is, you will also recognize that a new solution is inevitable and that it will be only a matter of time until it is in place. The question is no longer if these changes are going to happen, it is when they will happening.

We are in the midst of a transformational process, a massive paradigm shift in which our economic and financial system completely changes.

If you haven't felt the money pinch yet, this may all sound like a conspiracy to you. But it's not a conspiracy! The facts are on the table. The banks know - they can only play the game as long as the majority of us don't see how it's played. It's with every game you play, if you don't know all the rules and you haven't practiced it, you will always lose.

Do you remember playing Monopoly as a kid? Have you ever read the game manual? The most important sentence is the following: „The Bank can never go bankrupt"!

Now enjoy with me the fascinating ride through the money system - and I promise - at the end of this book, you will have gained freedom in your life around money you may never felt before. It's then up to you to put it into action. As an old native Indian saying goes: „If you see a problem and you don't do anything about it, you become part of the problem."

When a species is on the brink of destroying their habitat, they are either going extinct or they mutate. Given that our mind and the choice of free will is the latest advancement in our evolutionary path, I believe firmly that our thinking will mutate.

Change is the only constant in life, but we human beings are often trapped in the old habit and behavior to keep things as they are as a strategy to live and survive.

Many of the topics in this book are more or less a comprehensive summary. I intend to help you shift your awareness, so you see that you are a piece of a bigger puzzle. Use your talents and gifts, develop and cultivate them, and finally use them to create value for others. By doing so, you are creating abundance, and you will create wealth for yourself, for others and the world. Living from this mindset transforms darkness into light, and sadness into happiness and joy.

Chapter I - Where Does Money Come From?

The First Commodity Money

„Money is a new form of slavery, and distinguishable from the old simply by the fact that it is impersonal - that there is no human relation between master and slave." - Leo Tolstoy

A long time ago...

When people wanted to trade outside their tribe or village, they needed something; everyone could agree had value - something scalable - enter commodity monies. There were many kinds, but each had to embody the same five characteristics.

A commodity money is relatively scarce, easily recognizable, can be cut into smaller pieces. You can substitute one piece for another of equal value. And you can carry it around without too much trouble.

In ancient Rome, it was salt. The Aztecs used Cacao beans. It was whale teeth on Fiji. Yak dung in Tibet and shells in Africa and China. Grains, metal, ivory, rare stones, leather and fish. If it had the five characteristics of commodity money, someone probably used it as currency.

What value did these currencies have? If you go into a primary school, you'll see children exchanging rubber bands and Tamagotchi and Poke-man cards and baseball cards and sweets and candy and any other form of currency. People invent currency when they have no money.

About 2,500 years ago, the first metal coins were minted in China, and in what is now Turkey. These coins shared the same five characteristics with commodity money but were also very durable. In some cases, coins are the only thing left of entire civilizations.

Coins were an objective and universal unit of account, and they allowed people to buy and sell goods over vast regions. Coins worked, but only if people trusted that the king or emperor, who issued them, wasn't cheating on the metal content.

Using coins also meant, that an authority now controlled the supply of your currency. Money and political power were inextricably linked, centralized. Minting coins in a steady and predictable manner allowed economic growth and stability. The Wu Zhu coin in China retained its value for 500 years. In Constantinople, the solidus lasted for 700 years.

Do you remember what you learned in school about the Roman Empire? Probably nothing about their monetary system and how it collapsed.

When Julius Caesar first began minting large quantities of the aureus, it was 8 grams of pure gold. By the second century it had declined to 6.5 grams, and at the beginning of the fourth century, it was replaced by the 4.5-gram solidus. The purity of the coin itself was never debased, but the ever decreasing weight was a sure sign that government spending had been outpacing revenues for centuries.[3]

All of this, however, pales in comparison with the devaluation of the denarius. The denarius was the backbone of the Roman economy. Citizens earning their income in gold were a rarity given that a day's wage for an average laborer at the time is estimated at a single denarius. Thus it also became the target of severe abuse by the Roman authorities.

The denarius began as a 4.5 gram silver coin and stayed that way for centuries under the Roman Republic. After Rome became an empire, things began to turn sour for the denarius and, by extension, the Roman economy.

Base metals, such as copper were blended in with the silver and so even though the coin itself weighed the same, the amount of silver in it became less and less with each successive emperor.

Throughout the first century the denarius contained over 90% silver, but by the end of the second century, the silver content had fallen to less than 70%. A century later there was less than 5% silver in the coin, and by 350 AD it was all but worthless, having an exchange rate of 4,600,000 to a gold solidus - or nearly 9 million to the original aureus.

The economic chaos the hyperinflation had on the denarius and on the Roman society was devastating. The population of Rome reached a peak of about 1 million inhabitants during the first century BC and maintained that level until nearly the end of the second century. At this point, it began to decline throughout the third century slowly and precipitously throughout the fourth. By the fifth century, only about 50 thousand people remained.

Now let's jump forward to our time...

In the US throughout one of the worst financial crisis in 2008 many of the major 500 fortune companies received billions of dollars from the government - effectively provided by the taxpayers - to pay their employees and to survive. The real unemployment rate has not changed since then, only the formula how it is calculated. All major news companies in the US are using those new official numbers from the government and convince most of the public that the unemployment rate went down. Even as far down that, you may come to believe that the US has entered massive prosperity again - what a lie!

This massive bailout was one of the biggest charades the United States has ever seen.

Since then most salaries stagnated, and the middle class has vanished from the statistics. Once the cornerstone of a prosper economy, they now join the poor. In other words, the rich got richer, and the poor got poorer - and it's happening all over the world. This is the wealth gap and inequality, which is a primary cause of civil unrest starting all across the globe.

What Causes Inequality?

It's the result of the underlying mathematical economic formula, the base of our world financial system. All money that comes in circulation is debt - borrowed.

Governments are borrowing money from the banks, depositing it into central banks, then lending it to other banks, they create loans and within that process creating new money, and then lend it to corporation, businesses and individual people like you and me *with interest.*

History shows that this wealth gap usually represents the end of a monetary cycle. It commonly ends with a social revolution or a complete collapse of the economic system. We are precisely on this point right now, and the financial crash in 2008 was already an indicator of this end phase.

If you print additional money without an increase in goods and services, all money in the current market is devalued. It means that you suddenly can buy less even the $10 bill in your hand shows the same number on it. This process is called inflation, and it is the most potent and also hidden way of robbing your hard earned money.

Why would government borrow the money from the banks in the first place? Because most governments do not have any money and they are prohibited from creating their own money! If that all makes no sense to you, then the following story may shine some light on the history and creation of money.

The Story of the Goldsmith

„Money has never made man happy, nor will it, there is nothing in its nature to produce happiness. The more of it one has the more one wants." - Benjamin Franklin

The goldsmith was a practical man, and he observed the market very carefully. He quickly understood the inconvenience about dealing with large quantities of goods.

Remember, in the early days trading meant mainly to swap pigs for rugs and apples for bread. You had to go to distinct trading places and bring your complete assortment of production. It became very annoying and hindered the further expansion of trading.

The goldsmith came up with the brilliant idea to make small gold coins that would represent a specific value. Gold at his own has already value, so he just needed to produce coins with the right size. He would bring his idea to the Government for approval. Only those coins approved by the Government can be used and will have unique markings stamped on them. A brilliant idea.

Everybody could now obtain the number of gold coins they required from the goldsmith. There was no limit, except for the ability to repay. The more someone took, the more they must repay in one year's time.

Since the goldsmith provided the service, that is, the money supply, he thought he was entitled to payment for his work. For every 100 gold pieces someone obtains, they repay 105 for every year that they owe the debt. The extra five gold coins would be the additional charge, and the goldsmith called his charge interest.

After the coins were inspected and approved by the Governors, the system commenced. Some borrowed only a few, and they went off to try the new system. People found money to be marvelous, and they soon valued everything in gold coins. The value they placed on everything was called a „price," and the price mainly depended on the amount of work required to produce it. If it took a lot of work, the price was high, but if it was produced with little effort, it was inexpensive.

The Beginning of Competition

If more than one person provided the same product or service, only the price would distinguish them from each other. There was always the possibility to sell more goods when you lower the price. The moment one business lowered the price, the other business with the same product needed to reduce the price as well to stay in business. Prices came down - both businesses were striving to give the best quality at the lowest price. This behavior was genuine free competition.

The same happened to builders, transport operators, accountants, farmers, in fact, in every endeavor. The customers always chose what they felt was the best deal - they had freedom of choice. There was no artificial protection such as licenses or tariffs to prevent other people from going into business. The standard of living rose, and before long the people wondered how they had ever done without money.

At the end of the year, the goldsmith left his shop and visited all the people who owed him money. Some had more than they borrowed, but this meant that others had less, since there were only a certain number of coins issued in the first place. Those who had more than they borrowed paid back each 100 plus the extra 5, but still had to borrow again to carry on.

The Beginning of Debt

Others discovered for the first time that they had debt. Before he would lend them more money, the goldsmith took a mortgage over some of their assets, and everyone went away once more to try and get those extra five coins which always seemed so hard to find.

No one realized that as a whole, the country could never get out of debt until all the coins were repaid, but even then, there were those extra five on each 100 which had never been lent out at all. No one but the goldsmith could see that it was impossible to pay the interest.

The extra money had never been issued; therefore someone had to miss out.

It was true that the goldsmith spent some coins, but he couldn't possibly spend anything like 5% of the total economy on himself.

At the back of his shop, the goldsmith had a safe, and people found it convenient to leave some of their coins with him for safekeeping. He charged a small fee depending on the amount of money, and the time it was left with him. He would give the owner receipts for the deposit.

When a person went shopping, he did not usually carry a lot of gold coins. He would give the shopkeeper one of the receipts to the value of the goods he wanted to buy.

The Beginning of Currency

Shopkeepers recognized the receipt as being genuine and accepted it with the idea of taking it to the goldsmith and collecting the appropriate amount in coins. The receipts now passed from hand to hand instead of the gold. The people had great faith in the receipts - they accepted them as being as good as coins.

Note: The Dollar notes that you have in your wallet is not money, it is called currency. Money has real value – for example, a piece of gold is real money because it has intrinsic value. The Dollar note has no value at all – it's just the paper. The value is printed on it and represents an agreement on what it is worth.

The goldsmith noticed that it was quite unusual for anyone actually to ask for their gold coins. He realized that there might be dozens of people who would be glad to pay me interest for the use of this gold. It is rarely asked for and just lying here.

The gold does not belong to the goldsmith; however, it is in his possession. That gave him the idea that he hardly needs to make any coins at all, he can use some of the coins stored in his vault.

At first, the goldsmith was very cautious, only loaning a few at a time, and then only with high security. But gradually he became bolder, and he loaned out larger amounts.

People soon requested larger loans, and the goldsmith suggested that instead of carrying all these coins we can make a deposit in the name of the borrower, and then he gave several receipts to the value of the coins. The borrower went off only with a bunch of receipts. He had obtained a loan, yet the gold remained in the strong-room.

The goldsmith once again was very happy as he could "lend" gold and still keep it in his possession.

Friends, strangers, and even enemies needed funds to carry out their businesses - and so long as they could produce security, they could borrow as much as they needed. By merely writing out receipts. The goldsmith was able to "lend" money to several times the value of gold in his strong-room, and he was not even the owner of it. Everything was safe so long as the real owners didn't call for their gold and the confidence of the people was maintained.

He kept a book showing the debits and credits for each person. The lending business was proving to be very lucrative indeed. His social standing in the community was increasing almost as fast as his wealth. He was becoming a man of importance, and he commanded respect. In matters of finance, his word was like a sacred pronouncement.

Goldsmiths from other towns became curious about his activities and one day they called to see him. He told them what he was doing, but was very careful to emphasize the need for secrecy. If their plan were exposed, the scheme would fail, so they agreed to form their secret alliance. Each returned to his town and began to operate as the goldsmith taught.

How Checks Were Invented

People now accepted the receipts being as good as gold itself, and many receipts were deposited for safe keeping in the same way as coins. When a merchant wished to pay another for goods, he merely wrote a short note instructing the goldsmith to transfer money from his account to that of the second merchant. It took the goldsmith only a few minutes to adjust the figures.

This new system became very popular, and the instruction notes were called „checks". But there was a problem. Some people counterfeited the receipts...

In a meeting with all the Governors, the goldsmith stated that the receipts we issue have become very popular. No doubt, most of you Governors are using them, and you find them very convenient. However, some receipts were being copied by counterfeiters leaving out the goldsmith and his business model.

The Invention of Currency

The goldsmith suggestion that the Government's job should be to print new notes on a particular paper with very intricate designs, and then each note to be signed by the chief Governor. The Governors agreed as they thought that it is their job to protect the people against counterfeiters. So, they started to print the notes.

The goldsmith had another problem. Some people have gone prospecting and are making their gold coins for themselves. The goldsmith suggested to the government that a law should be passed so that any person who finds gold nuggets must hand them in. Of course, they will be reimbursed with notes and coins.

The idea sounded good, and without too much thought about it, the government printed a large number of crisp new notes. Each note had a printed value on it - $1, $2, $5, $10 etc. The goldsmiths agreed to pay for the additional small printing fee.

The notes were much more comfortable to carry, and they soon became accepted by the people. Despite their popularity, however, these new notes and coins were used for only 10% of transactions. The records showed that the check system accounted for 90% of all business.

The Next Plan of the Goldsmith

Until now, people were paying the goldsmiths to guard their money. To attract more capital into the vault, they offered to pay depositors 3% interest on their money.

Most people believed that the goldsmiths were re-lending their money out to borrowers at 5%, and his profit was the 2% difference. The people didn't question it, because getting 3% was far better than paying to have the money guarded.

The volume of savings grew, and with the additional money in the vaults, the goldsmiths were able to lend $200, $300, $400 sometimes up to $900 for every $100 in notes and coins that he held in deposit.

The goldsmith had to be careful not to exceed this nine to one ratio because one person in ten did require the notes and coins for use.

This system is now called officially „Fractional Reserve Landing Practice"

If there were not enough money available when required, people would become suspicious, especially as their deposit books showed how much they had deposited. Nevertheless, on the $900 in book figures that the goldsmith loaned out by writing checks to himself, he was able to demand up to $45 in interest, i.e., 5% on $900.

When the loan plus interest was repaid, i.e., $945, the $900 was canceled out in the debit column, and the goldsmith kept the $45 interest. He was therefore quite happy to pay $3 interest on the original $100 deposit which had never left the vaults at all. This meant that for every $100 he held in deposits, it was possible to make 42% profit, most people believing he was only making 2%. The other goldsmiths were doing the same thing.

They created money out of nothing at the stroke of a pen, and then charged interest on top of it.

True, they didn't coin money, the Government printed the notes and coins and gave it to the goldsmiths to distribute. The goldsmiths only expense was the small printing fee. Still, they were creating credit money out of nothing and charging interest on top of it.

Most people believed that the money supply was a Government operation.

People also believed that the goldsmiths were lending them the money that someone else had deposited, but it was bizarre that no one's deposits ever decreased when a loan was advanced. If everyone had tried to withdraw their deposits at once, the fraud would have been exposed.

When people requested additional loans in the form of notes or coins, the goldsmith explained to the Government that the increase in population and production would require more notes. The goldsmith again would cover the small printing fee.

The Problem With The Goldsmiths System

For every $100 the goldsmith issued, he was asking $105 in return. The extra $5 could never be paid back since it doesn't exist! You will, later on, see how this was one of the core issues that led to the global financial crisis of 2008 and the one that is still coming.

Farmers produce food, industry manufacturers goods, and so on, but only the goldsmith produces money. Suppose there are only two businessmen in the whole country and they employ everyone else. They borrow $100 each, pay $90 out in wages and expenses and allow $10 profit (their salary). That means the total purchasing power is $90 + $10 twice, i.e., $200.

To pay the goldsmith, they must sell their produce for $210. If one of them succeeds and sells all his goods for $105, the other business can only hope to get $95. Also, part of his products cannot sell, as there is no money left to buy them.

The business will still owe the goldsmith $10 and can only repay this by borrowing more. The system is impossible to work in the long-run.

The Scarcity of Money Begins

To succeed businesses must become more efficient, increase their production, cut down on expenses and become better in marketing and sales.

Most people respected the goldsmith's word. They seemed to be the expert, and the others must be wrong. The country developed and production has increased.

Merchants were forced to raise their prices to cover the interest on the money they had borrowed. Wage earners complained that wages were too low. Employers refused to pay higher wages to avoid ruin. Farmers could not get a fair price for their produce. Housewives complained that food was getting too expensive.

Finally, some people went on strike, a thing previously unheard.

Other people had become poverty stricken, and their friends and relatives could not afford to help them. Most had forgotten the real wealth all around - the fertile soils, the beautiful forests, the minerals, and cattle. They could only think about money, which always seemed so scarce.

They never questioned the system and still believed the Government was running it.

A few had pooled their excess money and formed "lending" or "finance" companies. They could get 6% or more this way, which was better than the 3% the goldsmiths paid, but they could only lend out money they owned - they did not have this strange power of being able to create money out of nothing by merely writing figures in books.

These finance companies worried the goldsmiths, so they quickly set up a few companies of their own. Mostly, they bought the others out before they got going. In no time, all the finance companies were owned by them, or under their control.

The economic situation was getting worse, and the wage earners complained that bosses were making too much profit. The bosses said that their workers were too lazy and weren't doing an honest day's work, and everyone was blaming everyone else. The Governors could not come up with an answer, and besides, the immediate problem seemed to be to help the poverty-stricken.

The Governors started up welfare schemes and made laws forcing people to contribute to them. Many people got angry - they believed in the old-fashioned idea of helping one's neighbor by voluntary effort.

These laws are nothing more than legalized robbery. Taking something from a person against his will, regardless of the purpose for which it will be used, is no different from stealing.

But most people felt helpless and afraid of the jail sentence, which was now punishment for failing to pay. These welfare schemes gave some relief, but very soon the problem was back, and more money was needed to cope.

The cost of these schemes rose higher and higher and the size of the Government grew!

Most of the Governors were sincere men trying to do their best. They didn't like asking for more money from their people, and finally, they had no choice but to borrow money from the goldsmiths. They had no idea how they were going to repay. Parents could no longer afford to pay teachers for their children. They couldn't pay doctors. Transport operators were going out of business.

One by one the government was forced to take these operations over. Teachers, doctors, and many others became public servants.

Few people obtained satisfaction in their work. They received a reasonable wage but lost their identity. They became small cogs in a giant machine. There was no room for personal initiative, little recognition for effort, their income was fixed, and advancement came only when a superior retired or died.

In desperation, the governors decided to seek the advice of the goldsmith. They suggested that the only way to balance things, is to take the excess wealth from the rich and give it to the poor.

Introduction of The Taxation System

The more a man has, the more he must pay. Collect taxes from each person according to his ability, and give to each according to his need. Schools and hospitals should be free for those who cannot afford it.

The goldsmith also mentioned to the government that they own them money. They've been borrowing now for quite some time. As they did not have all the money they borrowed, the goldsmith only agreed to get paid on the interest and the leave the principal still owned.

The government introduced the graduated income tax - the more you earn, the higher your tax rate. No one liked this, but they either paid the taxes or went to jail.

Merchants were forced once again to raise their prices. Wage earners demanded higher wages, which forced many employers out of business or to replace men with machinery. It caused additional unemployment and pushed the government to introduce further welfare and handout schemes.

Tariffs and other protection devices were introduced to keep industries and employment going. A few people wondered if the purpose of the production was to produce goods or merely to provide employment.

The situation got worse, and the government applied wage control, price control, and other sorts of restrictions. They also decided to get more money through sales tax, payroll tax and all kinds of taxes. Someone noted that from the wheat farmer right through to the housewife, there were over 50 taxes on a loaf of bread.

„Experts" arose and some were elected to Government, but after each yearly meeting they came back with almost nothing achieved, except for the news that taxes were to be „restructured," but overall the total tax always increased.

The goldsmiths began to demand their interest payments, and a larger and larger portion of the tax money was being needed to pay him.

The Party Politics Arrived

The people started arguing about which group of governors could best solve the problems. They argued about personalities, idealism, party labels, everything except the real problem. The councils were getting into trouble.

In some areas of the country, the interest on the debt exceeded the number of rates which were collected in a year. Throughout the land the unpaid interest kept increasing - interest was charged on unpaid interest.

Gradually much of the real wealth of the country came to be owned or controlled by the goldsmith and his friends, and with it came greater control over people. However, the thirst for power was not yet complete.

The goldsmith knew that the situation would not be secure until every person was under their control.

People opposing the systems could be silenced by financial pressure, or suffer public ridicule. To do this the goldsmith and his friends purchased most of the newspapers, T.V. and radio stations and he carefully selected people to operate them. Many of these people had a sincere desire to improve the world, but they never realized how they were being used. Their solutions always dealt with the effects of the problem, never the cause.

There were several different newspapers - one for the right wing, one for the left wing, one for the workers, one for the bosses, and so on. It didn't matter much which one you believed in, so long as you didn't think about the real problem.

The plan of the goldsmith was almost at its completion - the whole country was in debt to them. Through education and the media, they had control of people's minds. They were able to think and believe what they wanted them to.

After a man has far more money than he can spend for pleasure, what is left to excite him? For those with a ruling class mentality, the answer is power - raw power over other human beings. The idealists were used in the media and government, but the real controllers that the goldsmiths sought were those of the ruling class mentality.

Throughout the land, the goldsmith and his friends owned many lending offices. They were privately and separately owned. In theory, they competed with each other, but in reality, they were working very closely together. After persuading some of the governors, they set up an institution which they called the *Money Reserve Center*.

They didn't even use their own money to do this - they created credit against part of the money out of the people's deposits. This new institution gave the outward appearance of regulating the money supply and being a government operation, but strangely enough, no governor or public servant was ever allowed to be on the board of directors.

The government no longer borrowed directly from the goldsmith but began to use a system of I.O.U.'s to the Money Reserve Center. The security offered was the estimated revenue from next year's taxes.

This method was in line with the goldsmith's plan - removing suspicion from themselves to government operation. The goldsmiths were in control of the money, the lifeblood of the nation.

The government obtained the money, but interest was always charged on every loan. More and more was going out in welfare and handout schemes, and it was not long before the government found it difficult even to repay the interest, let alone the capital.

The administrations changed, the party labels changed, but the major policies continued. Regardless of which Government was in „power," the goldsmith's ultimate goal was brought closer each year. The people's opinions and outcry meant nothing. They were taxed to the limit, and they could pay no more.

The Goldsmiths Next Move – The Credit Card

10% of the money supply was still in the form of notes and coins. This had to be abolished in such a way as not to arouse suspicion. While the people used cash, they were free to buy and sell as they chose - they still had some control over their own lives. But it was not always safe to carry notes and coins. Checks were not accepted outside one's local community, and therefore a more convenient system was looked forward to.

Once again the goldsmith had the answer. Their organization issued everyone with a little plastic card showing the person's name, photograph, and an identification number.

When this card was presented anywhere, the storekeeper phoned the central computer to check the credit rating. If it was clear, the person could buy what he wanted up to a certain amount.

In the beginning, people were allowed to spend a small amount on credit, and if this was repaid within a month, no interest was charged. It worked well for the wage earner, but what businessman could even begin with this little amount? He had to set up machinery, manufacture the goods, pay wages, etc. and sell all his products and repay the money. If he exceeded one-month re-payment, he was charged 1.5% for every month the debt was owed.

This amounted to over 18% per year!

People in business had no option but to add the 18% onto the selling price. This extra money or credit (18%) had not been loaned out to anyone. Throughout the country, people in business had the impossible task of repaying $118 for every $100 they borrowed. Keep in mind that the extra $18 did not exist in the system.

The goldsmith and his friends increased their standing in society. They were regarded as pillars of respectability. Their pronouncements on finance and economics were accepted with almost religious conviction.

Under the burden of ever-increasing taxes, many small businesses collapsed. Special licenses were needed for various operations so that the remaining ones found it very difficult to operate.

The goldsmiths owned and controlled all of the big companies which had hundreds of subsidiaries.

These appeared to compete with each other, yet they controlled them all. Eventually, all competitors were forced out of business. Plumbers, panel beaters, electricians and most other small industries suffered the same fate - they were swallowed up by the goldsmith's giant companies which all had government protection.

This story is - of course - simplified, but reflects precisely where we are regarding money, and how we are all in debt by the system. Now you also understand that money is debt and each time you borrow money from the bank the amount of money (debt) increases in the system. That also means that if all debt were paid back, no more money would be existing!

Into the Financial Rabbit Hole

„If the practice persists of covering government deficits with the issue of notes, then the day will come without fail, sooner or later, when the monetary systems of those nations pursuing this course will break down completely. The purchasing power of the monetary unit will decline more and more, until finally it disappears completely."
- Ludwig von Mises, Austrian School economist

The financial system worldwide is in severe trouble, but why can't you read this in the news? Because already in the year 2000, half or more of the media businesses were owned by only six corporations interlocked with major commercial banks.

In designing the constitution of the United States, the Founding Fathers left out on purpose the federal income tax. The absence of the income tax allowed the economy to grow and its citizen to prosper for over a century.

The first national income tax was imposed in 1862. It was indented to fund the war between the States. It was only 3% and applied only to people that had an income of over $800, which at that time was less the one percent.

The tax return was only one page long and the tax code itself 14 pages in length. The tax code is now more than 17,000 pages. It has become so complex and complicated that over 250 billion is paid annually for tax services. The IRS has more than 144,000 workers currently. More than all of the largest corporations in America and employees, and more investigators than the FBI and the CIA combined.

An average of more than 40% of your income goes now away for taxes.

The federal income tax was designed to pay the interest that the government has to pay the Fed for lending it its money. In other words, all individual income tax revenues are gone before any nickel is spent on the services which you expect from your government. Next time you pay your taxes have this information in your mind.

The creation of money is a total mystery to probably 99 percent of the US citizens, which includes the people in the Congress and the Senate. The takeover of the US money creation by the Fed is one of the most mysterious acts in the US history.

If the government continues with the current rate of creating new debt then by 2018, it will have to raise the personal income tax to 70 percent. That is to pay the interest on the national debt. Not one cent goes into the educations system or any other social entity that creates our society and living standard.

The current Federal US debt - as of early 2018 - is about 20,6 trillion dollars.

A Free Economy Has Constant Deflation

The official economic definition of deflation means the lowering of the costs of goods and services. Deflation can happen if the yearly inflation rate drops to lower than zero percent, thereby creating a negative inflation rate.

The result of deflation is an actual gain in the purchasing power of your money, which means that the same quantity of dollars will purchase a higher number of such goods and services than it did previously. It is accurate to say that deflation increases your money's real value in the national economy.

In simple words, when there is the presence of deflation, your money will buy more, your wealth increases, and you might not have to work as many hours to pay your bills.

Without a governments interference, a healthy economy has persistent deflation.

Again, deflation means your money will buy more over time and your wealth increases. We had seen this scenario in history several times. Even in the medieval ages, we had a period of a few hundred years where people had more time and a better lifestyle than now. In a healthy economy, which is not manipulated by government, productivity increases over time. It leads to more an better products which can be bought with less money.

Let us assume you live in a village and there are 100 dollars in money circulating for 100 apples in productivity. At this point, an apple cost you one dollar. Over the years productivity usually increases and machines are developed to help with the harvest, transportation, and packaging of the apples. The price of apples goes down because less labor is required. There may also be more apples because of more sophisticated agriculture methods. Over the years you may only pay 50 cents for an apple, and you have money left over for other things. Of course, there is a limit here, especially when we talk about food production. But think about electronics and computers, which can now be produced almost entirely without the help of labor, and therefore the cost of production eventually goes to zero!

Besides, that labor that has been saved for the apple production now becomes available for other productivities and continues to improve the overall economy. Again, this scenario will occur only when the government does not intervene.

It's like a heroin addict, trying to kick the habit who shoots up each time any withdrawal symptoms set in. It's a painless way to go, but one unlikely to produce a healthy outcome.

The United States has become a country of consumers instead of producers and therefore destroys wealth instead of creating it. By borrowing to finance consumption, instead of saving to fund production, the US digs itself into an economic black hole - more profound than any other nations ever in history.

Borrowing to produce is the way a developing country becomes rich. Borrowing to consume is the way a rich country becomes poor.

The Fed is a cartel. By definition, a cartel is a group of independent businesses, which join together to coordinate the production, pricing, or marketing of their members. The purpose of a cartel is to reduce competition and thereby increase profitability. It is accomplished through a shared monopoly over their industry, which forces the public to pay higher prices for their goods or services as otherwise required under free market competition.

It is essential to understand that banks do not want you to pay back your loan. They are making a profit from the interest on the loan, not the repayment of the loan. If a loan is paid off, the bank has to find another borrower. One of the reasons banks prefer to loan to the government is that they do not expect those loans ever to be paid back.

Inflation is a Hidden Tax

The government uses Fiat money (currency without intrinsic value that has been established as money) to obtain instant purchasing power without taxation. However, the question remains where this purchasing power comes from. Since Fiat money is not backed up by anything of value like gold or silver as it used to be, the purchasing power can only come from subtracting it from somewhere else. In fact, it is collected from all citizens through the decline in purchasing power. It is, therefore, the same as a tax, but it is hidden and therefore operates silently behind the curtain.

Money is created at the moment it is borrowed. It is the act of borrowing which causes it to spring into existence. And the action of paying off the debt causes it to vanish.

Why Was the Fed Created?

The constitution of the United States prohibits both the states and the federal government from issuing Fiat money. It was a deliberate intent of the founding fathers who had already experienced the harsh effects of Fiat money before - especially in the revolutionary war. Creating the Fed as an independent entity that borrows the money to the government cleverly outmaneuvers the constitution.

The idea of being able to create prosperity by merely creating more money has always fascinated politicians and businessman. In every case that has been tried in history, the long-term consequences lead to the destruction of the economy and later on to falling society.

Our Education Model is Outdated

Our educational system is still to this date based upon the beginning of the industrial age. The objective is to use the classroom to teach attitudes that encourage people to be passive citizens who are educated enough for productive work under supervision, but not enough to question authority or seek to rise above their class.

Every time a teacher brings in a banker or a financial planner in a classroom in the name of financial education, they are allowing the fox to enter the henhouse. Instead of financial education young people get brainwashed to work for the banks. They learn how to open a bank account and to balance a check, but they will not learn how to build wealth for themselves and their families.

The word „educate" comes from the Latin term, which means „to draw out." Nothing else than engaging a student to find their solution and draw their conclusions. Just the opposite of what is taught today. On top of it, the current system teaches us to be lazy. We have someone else think for us and adapt their beliefs instead of making an effort to think on our own and come up with our unique answer.

There is a difference between having thoughts and thinking!

Let's dive into it...

The Banks Holy Grail - The Magic of Interest

„The process by which banks create money is so simple that the mind is repelled." - John Kenneth Galbraith, Canadian-born economist

The monetary system today is much more complicated than in the Goldsmith story. However, it still operated precisely on these principles. The complexity that has been added over the last 20-30 years ensures even more profit for the banks. The money schemas are now so convoluted that you need a bunch of financial lawyers and mathematicians to sieve through stacks of paper and complex formulas to understand how money is created out of thin air.

If the majority of the people understood the system, it would not last a day longer!

This financial setup created a winner-loser game. The biggest losers in this game are the Third World countries, as they have been seduced into opening their financial markets to currency manipulation. They have become helpless to the IMF or World Bank as they can now control their currency and run them into ever increasing debt amounts.

If you followed the goldsmith story, what do you think is the major problem that created all the other issues? Yes, it's the interest factor. The interest factor combined with the central banking system creates scarcity because it limits the abundance of money.

Another word for interest is usury, and people dealing with it are also called money changers. Usury is defined today as the practice of making unethical or immoral monetary loans that unfairly enrich the lender.

Originally, usury meant interest of any kind.

A loan may be considered usurious because of excessive or abusive interest rates or other factors. Historically in Christian societies, and in many Islamic nations today, charging any interest at all would be considered usury. Someone who practices usury can be called a usurer, but a more common term in contemporary English is a loan shark.

James Madison said that history records show, that the money changers have used every form of abuse, intrigue, deceit, and violent means possible to maintain their control over governments by controlling money and its issuance.

As money gets created out of thin air, it can be produced in unlimited quantities! Why then does printing trillions of dollars not create economic abundance? It seems the more gets printed, the worse it gets, and the less is available for the average person.

Money springs into existence by creating debt. All money is borrowed and has to be paid back plus interest. As the debt increases, the interest gets larger by every year and has to be extracted from products and services in the economy. It's an endless inclining spiral to death as it consumes until nothing is left.

It's the reason why we now have to pay for bottled water, for luggage on airline flights, checking accounts, coffee refills, information calls, parking, child care, TV. We always have to find new free resources and convert them into money. The latest edition is called „the sharing economy." By the way, sharing, in this case, means you have to pay. Services like Airbnb and Uber are monetizing one of our last free resources. We used to have a guest room for friends, and now they get booked for a fee. We used to have carpools with our co-workers, they now get charged for their ride.

Our freedom shrinks with each new service that monetizes something that used to free. Life used to be free not so long ago. Now we have to make a living!

The massive trillion dollar bailout of 2008 was not a bailout to help the businesses and the people. It was a bailout for the banks because they had loaned out too much money. Again, I am simplifying here as many other factors caused this financial disaster.

That's why the whole world is listing when the Federal Reserve makes its statement every week. Every word of the report gets dissected and interpreted from thousands of so-called financial experts. What everybody is looking for, is a sign of how the economy is doing, and if there are changes to the interest rate.

In a Nutshell

Governments borrow money from Banks. Banks are private institutions of rich people that make sure that governments are not allowed to print or establish money on their own. For the government to borrow the money, the banks charge interest. The interest has to be paid back by the end of the year on top of the loan. The bank, of course, is not interested that the loan gets paid back as otherwise, the interest payments vanish. As the banks create the loan out of thin air, they make a fortune on the interest payments!

If the government would do a good job, they could pay back the loan by the end of the year. However, they would still have to come up with the interest payment. There are several ways the governments could accomplish this:

- Higher taxes
- Higher fees
- Higher productivity
- Charging for something that was free before
- Debasing the currency (inflation)

Now you may understand why all politicians and news corporation continuously talk about GDP (Gross domestic product). The GDP has to go up every year to pay back the interest.

The whole story of constant growth and productivity is rooted in the simple fact of interest!

Governments Like Warfare - Guess Who Pays For It?

„A nation that continues year after year to spend more money on military defense than on programs of social uplift is approaching spiritual doom." - Martin Luther King, Jr.

Governments always wanted to take the people's money to finance its wars. That's mainly the history of money. Money and warfare go together. War is expensive. One year's income taxes aren't enough. Kings and queens had to borrow money against future taxes. They needed a groundbreaking financial innovation, government bonds.

The loans came from affluent merchant families and goldsmiths, who by now had become powerful financiers and bankers. Sovereign debt and deficit spending had been born.

In 1694, the bank of England was established to fund the war against France. England's central bank was privately owned and granted the monopoly to issue banknotes, a paper that could be redeemed for an equal amount of gold from the government's coffers. The central bank soon also managed the entire debt of the crown. Money has been a tool of sovereignty (supreme power or authority) for centuries.

Being able to issue currency gave you power, but it also gave the value to that monetary supply by backing it with the force of the state, which is essentially the debt of the state. When the U.S. won independence from Britain, the first article of the new constitution gave Congress the exclusive right to „coin money."

This currency's value was tied to gold in government vaults. From 1781 until the panic of 1907, the financial system of the U.S. was an economic „fruit basket." Brief central banks, state banks, private banks, private currency, government currency, depressions, vigorous growth, recessions, regular boom and bust cycles.

In 1913, bankers and politicians decided that it was in the country's best interest, and theirs, to have a permanent central bank. They created the Federal Reserve. Among its jobs, expand or contract the supply of a single national currency, the Federal Reserve note. The dollar was tied to gold, and strategic control of it would avoid booms that lead to busts. At least that was the plan. Then came the year 1929. The great depression would have a profound effect on monetary policy worldwide.

Soon, the Fed had printed nearly all the money it legally could to pump life back into the economy. It needed gold to fire up the mint. So in 1933, President Roosevelt issued a controversial executive order, forcing all U.S. citizens to sell their gold to the Federal Reserve at a fixed price, or go to prison.

The Fed offered far more cash to foreign governments for their gold. Many jumped at the offer. Gold flowed in, and dollars spread across the globe. World War II devastated nearly every major economy, except the United States. The military and industrial juggernaut emerged as the global financial superpower.

The dollar had become the world's most stable and trusted currency. Other countries pegged their currency to the dollar, which could still be redeemed for gold. In fact, the U.S. owned more than half of the world's gold reserves.

In the next few decades, more dollars were flowing to foreign countries. Governments began debasing their coins with cheaper metals and printing more of their own currency than they had in gold.

The bond between precious metals and paper currency was cracking. The 1966 50 cent piece was the last coin in regular circulation in Australia to contain silver. It included 80% silver, in 1966, this was 50 cents. Nowadays it's 8 dollars, roughly, in silver alone.

By 1966, foreign nations had had enough of the U.S. collecting gold and printing cash. They had more value in dollars than the U.S. had bullion in its vaults. They demanded gold in return for their paper dollars. Arguments about the value of the dollar versus their currency ensued.

In 1971, President Nixon settled the matter. He severed United States' currency from the gold standard. Never again could anyone legally demand U.S. Government gold in exchange for paper dollars. For better or worse, the dollar was now backed solely by the full faith and credit of the United States Government. The wealthiest nation the world had ever known would bet its future on a single word, trust.

Today the United States pays more than 400 billion dollars in interest to its creditors, every year.

When a government spends more money than it collects in taxes, it merely borrows more, or it creates more. At one time, every piece of paper money was backed by gold. For every 20 dollar bill, there was $20 worth of gold in a government vault. Not anymore.

Today, governments create currency by first creating bonds or treasury bills. These bonds are sold in the market, generating funds for the government that issued them. Large banks buy U.S. bonds to flip them, selling them to the Federal Reserve at a profit. This is how the magic money machine works.

The Fed is America's central bank. But it is not federal, doesn't have any money, and no cash on its balance sheets.

Since 1913, when the Federal Reserve took over the United States dollar, we've seen that the United States dollar has decreased in value 98%. Inflation is a far higher tax because on your income you pay it just once. If inflation is 2%, you're paying a 2% tax on your net worth every single year. The net worth that you held in currency.

If you earned a dollar in 1913, you could buy 16 loaves of bread. Today, a dollar barely buys you one. That's not a quaint notion of how cheap things used to be. It's proof that the value of your cash is slowly withering away. The U.S. dollar has gone from being worth one dollar to now being worth about 4 cents, so that's 96% of its original value. That's a direct result of government control.

What Really Happened in 2008?

The last financial crisis in 2008 had everything to do with virtual dollars. The banks sold more and shakier loans for a vast profit. They bundled those loans into packages, approved them with a triple-A rating and sold them to other investors. These loans are also called derivatives - nothing more than a huge legal scam.

A derivative is an asset that derives from another source. For example, you have an orange tree, and you create the orange juice from it. Then you ensure the production of this orange juice for the next year and sell this insurance to an investor.

Selling bad loans was a good business until the whole thing blew up in a global financial crisis. The magic money machine destroyed 30 million real jobs. The United States alone lost 16 trillion dollars in household wealth. The banks foreclosed on more than 1 million homes.

Selling subprime loans and betting they will fail, may not be sacred, but it is lucrative. As much as a quarter of our best and brightest people are being lured by the siren call of the money machine. Instead of science, engineering, or medicine, which could create new wealth, they chose a career playing with, betting with, other people's money to get rich quick and destroy wealth.

In Medieval Europe, a banker who couldn't repay depositors was hanged. Today, that same banker would get bailed out, paid bonuses and enjoy some tax benefits, too. To date, no senior U.S. banking executive has been charged for selling the bad loans that fueled the great recession.

In December 2014, just six years after the last banking crisis brought the world to its knees, a Congressman snuck a last-minute provision, written by Citigroup into a crucial funding bill. This rule allows the largest U.S. banks to make risky derivatives bets with bank deposits once again. However, no need to worry, if the banks implode again, lost deposits must be paid back by U.S. taxpayers - you!

Now Donald Trump rolled back some of the bank regulations that Obama put into place to restrict the power of the banks - setting up the stage for the next crash to come.

Destructive Results of the Current Monetary System

„War, poverty, corruption, hunger, misery, human suffering will not change in a monetary system. That is, there will be very little significant change. It's going to take the redesign of our culture and values."
- Jacque Fresco, American futurist & social engineer

The current monetary system results in a wide array of adverse social, environmental and economic consequences: high house prices, high public and private debts, inequality, declining environment and democracy, periodic booms & busts, and occasionally financial crises, depressions and even debt deflations, as well as severe consequences for growth, unemployment and investments. Worst of all, a decline of spiritual value and therefore more dissatisfaction, depression, moral decline, conflict, and war. [4]

Ever Increasing Debt

Most of the money is created by banks when they make loans. The only way to get extra money into the economy is to borrow it from banks, leaving us all trapped under a mountain of personal debt and mortgages.

Ever Increasing Costs of Products & Services

As more money needs to get created out of thin air, the value of money that's currently in the market deflates. Increasing the price of the products when you have more money would not be a problem. However, you never get an increase in salary that matches the increase in the prices of goods and services. You are ending up with paying more and having less.

Many of us were told that house prices are so high because there are too many people and not enough houses. While this is true, house prices have also been pushed up by the hundreds of billions of dollars of new money that banks created in the years before the financial crisis.[5] 99% of the money ends up in the hands of the top 5% rich, and they use it as an investment. It never trickles down to the workers.

Increasing Inequality

The fact that our money is issued as debt means that the level of debt must be higher than it otherwise would be. The interest that must be paid on this debt results in a transfer of wealth from the bottom 95% of the population (by income) to the top 5%, exacerbating inequality. This is the real reason for most conflicts and wars!

Environmental Decline

The impasse in our ability to convert nature into commodities and relationships into services is not temporary. There is little more we can convert. Technological progress and refinements to industrial methods will not help us take more fish from the seas - the fish are mostly gone.

It will not help us increase the timber harvest - the forests are already stressed to capacity. It will not allow us to pump more oil - the reserves are drying up. We cannot expand the service sector - there are hardly any things we do for each other that we don't pay for already. There is no more room for economic growth as we have known it; that is, no more room for the conversion of life and the world into money.[6]

There is nowhere to turn, we have reached the end of the line. Kicking down the can is no longer an option, as the can has now reached the end of the street.

Increasing Taxes & Fees

An ever-increasing amount of taxes and additional fees is needed to generate the extra interest money to pay back to the Fed. As the money supplies increases and the amount of interest grows, there will be a time not so far in the future, where all the taxes and fees cannot even amount to the outstanding interest fees. It's merely a mathematical equation and interesting enough we have almost reached that point by now. When this point is entered the government either has to declare national bankruptcy or borrows more money to be able to pay back the interest.

Increasing Job Loss

An ever-increasing competition between companies to produce more with less labor. When you see this in the long run, you understand that there will not be a secure job left in the future, as companies and corporations will do everything in their power to create more profit with less cost. Now you also understand why corporations always get bigger and form other alliances. It ensures the only way to generate more profit and satisfy all the stockholder and investors.

If corporations don't increase profit, they will be hammered by stock analysts. There rating goes down, and fewer people invest in the stock. The stock price falls, and again fewer people invest in the corporation. If the company continues with this scenario for a few quarters, it is already doomed to be bought by another.

For corporations to survive, they have to create a monopoly. Without having a monopoly you always have competition. Competition usually leads to lowers prices and profit margin, which further down the road leads either to bankruptcy or buyout of one of the competitors.

Before the Second World War ‚IG Farben' was the largest chemical company in the world and the fourth largest overall industrial concern after General Motors, U.S. Steel, and Standard Oil of New Jersey. Due to the company's entanglement with the Nazi regime, it was considered by the Allies to be too morally corrupt to be allowed to continue to exist. In the late 1940s, IG Farben was being rebuilt in the western zones and continue doing business. In 1951, the company was split into its original constituent companies. The four largest quickly bought the smaller ones. The successor companies again remain some of the world's largest chemical and pharmaceutical companies.

Stock analysts are not looking at the actual companies revenue. They are always looking for potential future revenue increase. It's the potential of what a company can create in future revenues that makes it attractive to investment brokers and stockholders.

Offering employment was never the intention of companies and corporations, that's just a form of propaganda. The sole purpose is to make money.

Increasing Competition

From the scarcity, that is built into the monetary system rises the physiological state of survival, which always produces the question: „What's in it for me?"

If you are making money by selling a particular product, you are automatically going to fight the existence of another product that may threaten your business. This issue alone undermines the natural flow of being fair to each other. We start not to trust each other anymore.

Someone may come over to you and say: „I've got just the house you're looking for." However, you immediately have to be aware that this person may be a salesman. Because of that, the house may not be what you are looking for. It may only add monetary value to the person who wants to sell it to you. Maybe that person is entirely motivated by the commission he may get.

When a doctor tells you: „I think your kidney has to come out." You don't know if he's trying to pay off a yacht or is financing his new home or car. This monetary system makes it very hard to trust people. The financial system is not designed to serve the well-being of people.

Even this all sounds like terrible news, and it makes you feel angry it is a necessary step to make you understand the foundation of money. The worst thing you can do right now is hating the banks and the governments. Yes, the truth is hard to swallow, but making them responsible will not empower you, it will make you a victim of the circumstances. As long as each of us makes their first decision about the money we will all continue to feed the system.

Now that you know how money works you can make different decisions. You now also understand that the system is either going to fail or will undergo significant changes. The financial crisis of 2008 was just the peak of the iceberg.

For now, that's all you need to understand. In some of the later chapters, I will provide you with more details, and what better choices you can make. Also, why your beliefs and actions around money will make all the difference in your life.

Moral Decline

We can already see that the motivation and morale of many young people are going to zero. Who can blame them? They can sense somehow or be able to understand that they have no future, that the whole system has nothing exciting to offer. They look around, and they find no vision that they can align. They do not see any purpose to get a job that leads to nowhere.

Who wants to start a career with $50,00 - $100,000 in debt? To make people pay for education almost guarantees to create more thieves and bank robbers. It's a perfect set-up for creating more criminals and homeless people. That's why the war against drugs is a charade. It looks to the wrong place to solve the problem.

To charge people for education is a crime by itself because it forces and encourages people to fall into their dark side. It brings out the worst in people instead of cultivating the good. People are not born evil, they pick it up from society.

Health Decline

As mentioned before, corporations are forced by the financial system to have only one goal, and that is to increase profit. If they don't, they get slammed by the shareholders and stock analysts.

More profit is only possible by producing more and cheaper products. In the long run quantity over quality always wins. With decreasing quality products lasts shorter and ultimately destroy more and more environment by using more resources and producing more toxic landfill.

One of the most sensitive areas in our lives is food. Food that is more and more produced by big corporations becomes so low on nutritional value that it could hardly be called food anymore. Besides that, the artificial and chemical ingredients that are necessary to add artificial flavoring are also causing significant health problems.

With skyrocketing rises in heart diseases and diabetes, individual companies can produce ever-increasing profits. Remember, that the GDP also counts the sick people and their treatments!

Did you know that 99% of cancer and diabetes can be avoided and also healed in early stages by merely changing your diet? You usually will not hear about this, until you do your research. There is nothing earned for the pharmaceutic industry when you eat healthily and be healthy.

More people will get sick by ever increasing stress and unable to work. They may not be even able to pay for medication. Who is going to create anything of value at this point? Who is adding any wealth to the system? The whole system has to come to a complete collapse sooner or later. Think about it!

Spiritual Decline

According to just published data[7], 12.7 percent of Americans age 12 or older reported taking an antidepressant within the last month.. The shadow numbers are probably going as high as 40%-50% when you take into account alcohol, and drug consumes.

Using medication is a way out for people to escape the pressure, the stress, and not having a purpose in life. Interesting enough, from a psychology point of view, it is an indication to connect with the spiritual world. It's an unconscious way of zooming out, expanding from a feeling of narrowness, restriction, and contraction. Most people are not aware of this fact; otherwise, they could use different outlets to accommodate this desire. The primary hope is to move away from discomfort. It's not a conscious decision to create comfort.

A recent statistic showed that 69% of Americans have less than $1000 in their bank account when they die. Another one said that 99.9% of people had not accomplished their dream in life when they die.[8]

How many places in our world are left to find spiritual connection besides the church? However, even with the church, many people feel that the church is stuck in the past. Instead of being supportive, it's another way of indoctrination.

There is a growing field of spiritual literature and workshops available but for most people that means a financial investment. So here we are again – paying for our education.

and the list goes on...

- Undermining Democracy
- Increased Bureaucracy
- Loss of Freedom
- More Laws & Regulations
- More Prisoners and Crime

- More and longer Recessions
- More Bankruptcies
- Depletion of Resources
- Loss of Nature & Life
- Increasing Isolation
- Increasing Fear

In the next few chapters, I will guide you through the most common robbing methods the current monetary system has in place to steal your hard-earned money. The first few methods may be evident to you, but you will be astonished how the banks and the governments pull it off.

After the obvious ones, you will find several other methods, which may seem to you as not related to money. However, you will soon recognize that these hidden methods have even more power to steal your money than the ones explained in the beginning.

Chapter II - Methods That Legally Steal Your Money

Robbing Method #1 - The Federal Reserve

„There are two ways to conquer and enslave a nation. One is by the sword and the other is by debt." - President John Adams

The Federal Reserve System is commonly referred to as the Fed. This body functions as the United States central banking system. As a result of many financial waves of panic that rocked the U.S. from the late 1800's through an unusually harsh panic in 1907, Congress enacted the Federal Reserve Act in 1913.

The Great Depression first led to the expansion of powers and roles of the Federal Reserve System. From a primary role as central banker to the United States, the organization has evolved to its status today as the overseer of the country's financial system stability. Also, as a conductor of the country's monetary policy, regulator and supervisor of the banking system and institutions, and provider of critical financial services to the banks, savings and loan companies, foreign banks, and the Federal government.

The Federal Reserve is not federal, and it keeps no reserve. The only thing you could call reserve are some bookkeeping entries. However, you can't find money or gold there.

The Federal Reserve commonly called the "Fed" is by most people confused with the U.S. Government, but it is private corporation. It is so secret that its stock is not even traded on the stock exchange market. A consortium of private banks owns it. The biggest of which are Citibank and J.P. Morgan Chase Company.

The head of the Fed can be reappointed indefinitely and answers to no one. It is entirely independent of oversight and any government control. The Federal Reserve is, in short, the total money-making machine. Whenever the government needs money, they need to ask the Fed. The Fed then issues a particular check (so-called bond) to the government. Simply put, the government owes that money to the Fed.

The federal government gives U.S. Treasury bonds to the Federal Reserve, and the Federal Reserve gives the U.S. government "Federal Reserve Notes" in return. Usually, this is done electronically.

The act of writing this special check creates money out of thin air – it did not exist before! It is a debt spiral that is designed to go on perpetually.

The money supply is designed to expand under the Federal Reserve system constantly. That is why we have all become accustomed to thinking of inflation as "normal."

What does the Federal Reserve do with the U.S. Treasury bonds that it gets from the U.S. government? It sells them off to others. There are lots of people that have made money by holding U.S. government debt. In fiscal 2016, the U.S. government paid out 432 billion dollars just in interest on the national debt. In 2017 until October the sum is already 404 billion dollars.

In 2016 that was 432 billion dollars that were taken out of our pockets and put into the pockets of wealthy individuals and foreign governments around the globe.

The Federal Reserve Destroys the Value of The U.S. Dollar

Did you know that the U.S. dollar has lost 96.2% of its value since 1900? Of course, almost all of that decline has happened since the Federal Reserve was created in 1913.

Because the money supply is designed to expand continuously, it is guaranteed that all of our dollars will steadily lose value. Inflation, therefore, is a "hidden tax" that continually robs us all of our wealth.

Finance Government Debt with Personal Income Tax

Do you think it was an coincidence that we saw the personal income tax and the Federal Reserve System both come into existence in 1913? On February 3rd, 1913 the 16th Amendment to the U.S. Constitution was ratified. Later that year, the United States Revenue Act of 1913 imposed a personal income tax on the American people and we have had one ever since.

Without a personal income tax, it is hard to have a central bank. It takes massive amounts of money to finance all of the government debt that a central banking system creates.

The whole money system is built on debt. Starting with the Fed writing a check to the government and other private institutions. If there were no debts in our money system, there wouldn't be any money at all. That explains why the federal debt never gets paid off.

To pay off the debt would mean to destroy the money supply. In short - The Federal Reserve is a money-making machine. It is actually debt in form of currency and not money. Money or currency is an invention like inches or seconds. It is a man-made concept that has as much reality as we are making of it.

To sum up, the Federal Reserve is an independent, privately owned corporation with the purpose to create money out of nothing, lend it to the government at interest, and controls the nations money supply. Expanding or contracting it at free will.

Robbing Method #2 - Manipulating Interest Rates

"Compound interest is the eighth wonder of the world. He who understands it, earns it ... he who doesn't ... pays it." - Albert Einstein

The Fed also controls the expansion of the money supply by just raising and lowering the interest rates. A higher interest rate contracts the money supply and lower interest expands the money supply. When the interest rate is high, it costs you more to borrow money. When the interest rate is low, then you can borrow money cheaper.

A good example is a home mortgage. When interest rates are high, you may pay 12% interest on your mortgage, which means for every $100.000 you borrow you have to pay back $12.000 by the end of the year or $1000 per month. With low interest, you may only pay 5%, which comes to $5.000 per year or around $420 per month.

By manipulating this number, the Fed causes periods of booms and recessions continuously. If you create money from the money, you have not created additional value for the society. All the goods and services that are produced do not change when the Fed is changing the Interest rate. What that means is that the Fed has full control over the outcome of the economy at any given moment.

The Fed has created every boom and recession since 1913. Booms and depressions do not happen without reason, and they are not a typical appearance of a free and healthy economy.

There was a reason, that at the beginning of the monetary system, interest was not allowed. In the early ages, interest was called usury. Usury was forbidden in the Christian Bible, and the Catholic church strictly enforced usury laws. However in the Jewish scriptures usury was only banned between brothers. Charging interest to so-called for-eigners was allowed and legal. People that charged interest to others people by lending money were called 'moneychangers.' Later on the road, the principal of usury was ig-nored, and the kings as well as the church adopted it.

The main reason for making usury illegal is the expansion of the money supply without adding productivity or service to society. It's nothing else than a way of counterfeiting money. Let me explain this in a simple fictional scenario:

Let's assume you and 99 other people get stranded on an uninhabited island in the middle of the Pacific. You create your own small economy as you also have a chest of 1000 gold coins. To be fair each person gets 10 gold coins to start with. Everybody is prosperous and wealthy in the beginning.

You are voted to manage and oversee the trading with gold coins, and therefore you like to be paid. You are charging 10% interest per year on all 1000 gold coins you hand out to the 100 people including yourself. Let's fast forward to the end of year one.

You are supposed to get one gold coin from each person, which represents 10% inter-est. After year one you see that your little community has started to produce and trade. Not all of them, and some more than others. Some people gained gold coins, and oth-ers lost some due to not creating anything for various reasons.

Even if someone maintained their ten gold coins, he or she now has to give you one for the interest he or she owes you. You are taking in 100 gold coins, and your community has 100 gold coins less.

Fast forward to year five and the community is not doing so well. Again you are col-lecting your 100 gold coins from each person. At that point, the community money has decreased by 50%. There is less money available to pay for the goods and services that are offered. Some people have not even one coin left and are now starving. Others have gained a few coins, but see that in the long run, they will also run out of gold coins. The whole system collapses over time because the money that is needed to pay the interest does not exist in the system. It is taken from the money that is used to trade products and services. In the end, you have all the money like the banks do!

In short, this system creates scarcity and the direct consequence is that we have to fight with each other to survive!

In a Nutshell

By allowing a centralized authority such as the Federal Reserve to dictate interest rates, it creates an environment where financial bubbles can be formed relatively quick and easy.

Over the past several decades, we have seen bubble after bubble. Most of these have been the result of the Federal Reserve keeping interest rates artificially low. If the free market had been setting interest rates all this time, things would have never gotten so far out of hand.

For example, the housing crash would have never been so horrific if the Federal Reserve had not created such ideal conditions for a housing bubble in the first place. People could get loans with mainly no income and no money down - so-called Ninja loans.

The Federal Reserve continues to set interest rates much, much lower than they should be. It is causing a tremendous misallocation of economic resources, and there will be massive consequences for that down the line. In simple terms, we are seeing the wealth gap expanding until either the money system changes or until there is civil unrest.

Robbing Method #3 - Fiat Money

„It is well enough that people of the nation do not understand our banking and monetary system, for if they did, I believe there would be a revolution before tomorrow morning." - Henry Ford

The gold standard and Bretton Woods Agreements were the bedrock framework for the world financial system following the economic devastation of World War II. In this system of foreign exchange control, the dollar and other major world foreign currencies such as the British Pound, Swiss Franc, German Deutsche Mark, Canadian Dollar, French Franc, and others, all had values to the price of gold. It led to a generally stable international financial regime and economies.

By the time the 1970's arrived, the United States had reached the point that both increasing domestic program spending and the Vietnam War created a simultaneous trade deficit, and a deficit in the balance of payments. These proved to be the first in the entire twentieth century for America. In the year 1970, the dollar declined in gold coverage from fifty-five percent down to twenty-two percent, representing a staggering decline of thirty-three percentage points.

The End of the Gold Standard
You may recall that in the next year - 1971, the American government printed even more dollars to pay the domestic and military spending bills. Washington printed ten percent more dollars, which they dispatched overseas. Confidence in the U.S. dollar was quickly crumbling, as $22 billion in physical assets were withdrawn from the United States in only the first six months of the year.

The U.S. was not the first country to abandon the Bretton Woods agreement. West Germany made the first leap to avoid the inevitable inflation. They saw it coming through the U.S. economy and the declining dollar as a result of the reckless economic behavior that the U.S. had begun practicing.

After this, the other major economies of Western Europe started demanding more gold from the U.S. as a fulfillment of its promise to pay the bills. The U.S. gold reserves began sinking rapidly, as both Switzerland and France demanded hundreds of millions of dollars in gold.

Switzerland became the second country to leave the Bretton Woods agreement. Not to be outdone, and with the dollar tanking against other currencies and gold, President Richard Nixon finally decided to end the U.S. dollar to gold convertibility. In one swift move, he abandoned both, the gold standard and the Bretton Woods system, which more or less collapsed with the U.S. forsaking true gold accountability.

The Results of the U.S. Departing from the Gold Standard

The resulting chaos that wracked currencies and financial markets over the next ten plus years demonstrated what a radical decision of abandoning gold proved to be. Before Nixon withdrew from the dollar to gold convertibility agreement in 1971, the U.S. dollar stood at between $40 and $44 per ounce of gold. Within a year of Nixon leaving the gold standard in 1972, the dollar had dropped to an average of almost $64 per ounce.

It represented a staggering more than fifty percent drop in the value of the dollar in only that first year. The situation just became worse with time, as the dollar continued to crash and burn. 1973 saw an average gold price of $106.50 per ounce, 1974 witnessed $183 plus average cost per ounce, and by 1980 gold had risen to nearly $595 per ounce against the dollar. The other way of saying this is, of course, that the dollar had dropped from only $42 per ounce average in 1971 to $595 per ounce by 1980, representing an unbelievable over 1,300 percent drop in the dollar in less than ten years.

The dollar managed to stabilize in the next few decades, with gold fluctuating wildly over the next twenty or so years. The continuing decline of the dollar since Nixon abandoned the gold standard continues to this day.

2520% Inflation in 40 Years Is The Result

In 2009, the average gold price was $972, while the 2010 full year price is set to be over $1,100 per ounce. Since the gold standard and Bretton Woods agreement were discarded then, the U.S. dollar has collapsed from around $42 per ounce to more than $1,100 per ounce. It represents a crushing 2,520% in forty years. When you wonder how significant an event withdrawing from the gold standard and Bretton Woods treaty was, consider this:

The government publishes an inflation rate that averages two to four percent per year. Gold tells us that the dollar has dropped more than 60% per year on average over the last forty years. Leaving the gold standard caused a radical change in the financial world.

Abandoning the gold standard and backing up the dollar by gold has changed money into currency. What you are holding now in your pocket is no longer money. It is a worthless paper that you can only exchange for another paper. You are not in control of the value of that piece of paper. You can no longer go to the bank and demand to get gold for your dollar. This currency system is also called Fiat money.

The Fiat Currency System

A fiat currency is a currency that is not backed up by gold or any other value. Almost all currencies in use today are fiat currencies.

A fiat currency is designed to lose value. Its very purpose is to confiscate your wealth and transfer it to the government.

The currency game works against most people. The whole system is designed to transfer wealth from those who don't understand the system to those who do. Easy credit and the current fiat system are a tax on the poor and the middle class.

Let's say your income increases by 2% per year and the value of the dollar goes down by 8%. That means you lose 6% of your purchase power in one year! There are times in history where the dollar lost 3% in a few days, and you will see an even stronger decline in the future.

This lost purchase power is nothing else than a hidden tax on you. Because it happens gradually, you are not that much aware of it. You only realize that with every month your money buys less and it is just a matter of time until you have nothing left at all.

Robbing Method #4 - The Fractional Reserve Banking System

"By this means government may secretly and unobserved, confiscate the wealth of the people, and not one man in a million will detect the theft." - John Maynard Keynes, British economist

The next big trick the banks pull off is close to real magic. Remember the story with the goldsmith and the fact that they could loan money several times over because only in rare cases people wanted to get their money out of it. A majority of all business and people kept their money with the goldsmith indefinitely.

When you go to the bank and request a loan, the bank does not need to have this money. First, they issue you a promissory note in exchange for the credit. That means the bank claims part of your home, car or any other valuable good you may have. If you don't pay back the loan, they will get a part of your house, car or whatever you signed over to them in the promissory note.

Second, as you take out this new loan, you create debt. The surprising fact is, that the debt counts in the banks bookkeeping as a plus. The bank created the money again out of thin air. It comes even better. Now that the bank has established new money with your loan they can immediately start to loan that money to other people and create even more money. This is usually done ten times over as the bank is required to keep only a portion of the first debt as a reserve.

This gigantic magic trick is called fractional reserve banking, and it is the fundamental principle of how most banks in the world operate.

Can the banks make even more profit? Yes, because they charge you interest to take out the loan. So with every loan someone takes out, the bank not only create that money, they generate money on top with your interest payments. These interest payments alone are sometimes higher than the loan (principal) that you took out. That's the reason banks and credit card companies are not interested that you pay back your loan.

For instance, if you deposit $100,000 at the bank and the bank has a reserve requirement of 10 percent, the bank must keep $10,000 of your money on reserve and can lend out the $90,000. In essence, the bank has taken $100,000 and has turned it into $190,000 by giving you a $100,000 credit on your deposits, and then lending the additional $90,000 out to someone else.[9]

Now, if you take this out a little further, you will see that your original $100,000 can become 1 Million Dollar by the time it is all over. Here's how:

• You deposit $100,000, your bank loans someone else $90,000
• That person deposits $90,000, their bank loans someone else $81,000
• That person deposits $81,000, their bank loans someone else $72,900
• That person deposits $72,900, their bank loans someone else $65,610
• That person deposits $65,610, their bank loans someone else $59,049
• That person deposits $59,049, their bank loans someone else $53,144
• That person deposits $53,144, their bank loans someone else $47,829
• And so on...

Ultimately, your initial $100,000 can grow into $1,000,000 with a 10 percent reserve requirement. As you can also see in the goldsmith story, this money system is doomed to fail at one point. We observe an ever-increasing money supply, and that there is not enough money in the system to pay back the Fed. Remember that the interest on the original loan from the Fed is not created and therefore not in the money supply.

Robbing Method #5 - Taxes and Fees

„If you use money, you lose money" - Anonymous

An ever-increasing amount of taxes and additional fees is needed by the government to generate the extra interest money to the Fed. As the money supplies increases and the amount of interest grows, there will be a time not so far in the future, where all the taxes and fees cannot even amount to the outstanding interest fees. It's a fundamental mathematical equation and interesting enough the U.S. had already reached that point a long time ago. When this point arrives, the government either has to declare national bankruptcy or borrow more money to be able to pay back the interest. It's the money death spiral!

Every new president promises tax reduction because people always demand lower taxes. However, rest assured that after each election the taxes will increase one way or the other. If one tax gets lowered another tax will either grow, or a new tax or fee will be invented. The government and the media will inform you what taxes have been lowered. However, they will hide from you what taxes and fees go up.

In 2014 U.S. citizen spend more than 7 billion hours preparing their taxes and hand over more than four trillion dollars to federal, state and local governments. They forked over nearly 30 percent of what they earn to pay their income taxes, but that is only a small part of the story.

As you will see below (list provided by Michael Snyder), there are dozens of other taxes. Of course, not everyone pays all of these taxes, but without a doubt, we are all being taxed into oblivion. It is like death by a thousand paper cuts. Our politicians have become incredibly creative in finding ways to extract money from all of us, and most of us don't even realize what is being done to us.

By the time it is all said and done, a significant portion of the population ends up paying more than half of what they earn to the government. Nothing will be done about it until people start demanding change. The following is a list of 97 taxes U.S. citizens pay every year...

1. Air Transportation Taxes
2. Biodiesel Fuel Taxes
3. Building Permit Taxes
4. Business Registration Fees
5. Capital Gains Taxes
6. Cigarette Taxes
7. Court Fines (indirect taxes)
8. Disposal Fees
9. Dog License Taxes
10. Drivers License Fees (another form of taxation)
11. Employer Health Insurance Mandate Tax
12. Employer Medicare Taxes
13. Employer Social Security Taxes
14. Environmental Fees
15. Estate Taxes
16. Excise Taxes On Comprehensive Health Insurance Plans
17. Federal Corporate Taxes
18. Federal Income Taxes
19. Federal Unemployment Taxes
20. Fishing License Taxes
21. Flush Taxes (yes, this actually exists in some areas)
22. Food And Beverage License Fees
23. Franchise Business Taxes
24. Garbage Taxes
25. Gasoline Taxes
26. Gift Taxes
27. Gun Ownership Permits
28. Hazardous Material Disposal Fees
29. Highway Access Fees
30. Hotel Taxes
31. Hunting License Taxes
32. Import Taxes
33. Individual Health Insurance Mandate Taxes
34. Inheritance Taxes
35. Insect Control Hazardous Materials Licenses
36. Inspection Fees
37. Insurance Premium Taxes
38. Interstate User Diesel Fuel Taxes
39. Inventory Taxes
40. IRA Early Withdrawal Taxes
41. IRS Interest Charges (tax on top of tax)
42. IRS Penalties (tax on top of tax)
43. Library Taxes
44. License Plate Fees
45. Liquor Taxes
46. Local Corporate Taxes
47. Local Income Taxes
48. Local School Taxes
49. Local Unemployment Taxes
50. Luxury Taxes
51. Marriage License Taxes
52. Medicare Taxes
53. Parking Meters
54. Passport Fees
55. Professional Licenses And Fees (another form of taxation)
56. Property Taxes
57. Real Estate Taxes
58. Recreational Vehicle Taxes

59. Registration Fees For New Businesses
60. Toll Booth Taxes
61. Sales Taxes
62. Self-Employment Taxes
63. Sewer & Water Taxes
64. School Taxes
65. Septic Permit Taxes
66. Service Charge Taxes
67. Social Security Taxes
68. Special Assessments For Road Repairs Or Construction
69. Sports Stadium Taxes
70. State Corporate Taxes
71. State Income Taxes
72. State Park Entrance Fees
73. State Unemployment Taxes (SUTA)
74. Tanning Taxes (a new Obamacare tax on tanning services)
75. Telephone 911 Service Taxes
76. Telephone Federal Excise Taxes
77. Telephone Federal Universal Service Fee Taxes
78. Telephone Minimum Usage Surcharge Taxes
79. Telephone State And Local Taxes
80. Telephone Universal Access Taxes
81. The Alternative Minimum Tax
82. Tire Recycling Fees
83. Tire Taxes
84. Tolls (another form of taxation)
85. Traffic Fines (indirect taxation)
86. Use Taxes (Out of state purchases, etc.)
87. Utility Taxes
88. Vehicle Registration Taxes
89. Waste Management Taxes
90. Water Rights Fees
91. Watercraft Registration & Licensing Fees
92. Well Permit Fees
93. Workers Compensation Taxes
94. Zoning Permit Fees

This list is from 2014, and you can be sure it now runs past the number 100. Despite all of this oppressive taxation, your local governments, your state governments, and your federal government are all drowning in debt. When the federal income tax was initially introduced a little more than 100 years ago, most US citizens were taxed at a rate of only 1 percent.

Since that time, tax rates have gone much higher, and the tax code has exploded in size. The U.S. tax code is now 3.8 million words long. If you took all of William Shakespeare's works and collected them together, the entire collection would only be about 900,000 words long. 75 years ago, the instructions for Form 1040 were two pages long. Today, they are 189 pages long. There have been 4,428 changes to the tax code over the last decade. It is incredibly costly to change tax software, tax manuals and tax instruction booklets for all of those changes.

When the U.S. government first implemented a personal income tax in 1913, the vast majority of the population paid a rate of just 1 percent, and the highest marginal tax rate was only 7 percent.

Too Much Regulation Kills Innovation

Kids trying their first experiment with entrepreneurship are being shut down all over America. Opening a simple lemonade stand and selling lemons seems to be impossible these days. Jump with me through the legal hoops required to open a simple lemonade stand in New York City. Here's some of what one has to do:

1. Register as sole proprietor with the County Clerk's Office (must be done in person)
2. Apply to the IRS for an Employer Identification Number
3. Complete 15-hr Food Protection Course!
4. After the course, register for an exam that takes 1 hr. You must score 70 percent to pass. If you pass, allow 3-5 weeks for delivery of Food Protection Certificate.
5. Register for sales tax Certificate of Authority
6. Apply for a Temporary Food Service Establishment Permit. Must bring copies of the previous documents and completed forms to the Consumer Affairs Licensing Center.

Then, at least 21 days before opening your establishment, you must arrange for an inspection with the Health Department's Bureau of Food Safety and Community Sanitation. It takes about three weeks to get your appointment. If you pass, you can set up a business once you buy a portable fire extinguisher from a company certified by the FDNY and set up a contract for waste disposal.[10]

What do the kid's experience and what are their conclusion? Don't try anything on your own, better go to a place where someone has already established something - in other words, a job!

Robbing Method #6 - Bank Bailouts

„I believe that banking institutions are more dangerous to our liberties than standing armies. If the American people ever allow private banks to control the issue of their currency, first by inflation, then by deflation, the banks and corporations that will grow up around will deprive the people of all property until their children wake-up homeless on the continent their fathers conquered. The issuing power should be taken from the banks and restored to the people, to whom it properly belongs." - Thomas Jefferson, American Founding Father

During the last financial crisis, the Federal Reserve secretly conducted the biggest bailout in the history of the world, and the Fed fought in court for several years to keep it a secret.

Do you remember the TARP (Troubled Asset Relief Program) bailout? The American people were outraged that the federal government spent 700 billion dollars bailing out the "too big to fail" banks. Well, that bailout was pocket change compared to what the Federal Reserve did.

As you will see documented below, the Federal Reserve handed more than 16 trillion dollars in nearly interest-free money to the "too big to fail" banks between 2007 and 2010. The Federal Reserve has been actively picking "winners" and "losers" in the financial system, and it turns out that the "friends" of the Fed always get bailed out and always end up among the "winners."

According to the limited GAO audit of the Federal Reserve that was mandated by the Dodd-Frank Wall Street Reform and Consumer Protection Act, the total of all the secret bailouts conducted by the Federal Reserve during the last financial crisis comes to a whopping $16.1 trillion. Keep in mind that the GDP of the United States for the entire year of 2010 was only 14.58 trillion dollars.

Some other dollar figures have been thrown around lately regarding these secret Federal Reserve bailouts. Let's take a look at them and see what they mean.

According to the GAO audit, $16.1 trillion in secret loans were made by the Federal Reserve between December 1, 2007, and July 21, 2010. The following list of firms and the amount of money that they received was taken directly from page 131 of the GAO audit report.

- Citigroup – $2.513 trillion
- Morgan Stanley – $2.041 trillion
- Merrill Lynch – $1.949 trillion
- Bank of America – $1.344 trillion
- Barclays PLC – $868 billion
- Bear Sterns – $853 billion
- Goldman Sachs – $814 billion
- Royal Bank of Scotland – $541 billion
- JP Morgan Chase – $391 billion
- Deutsche Bank – $354 billion
- UBS – $287 billion
- Credit Suisse – $262 billion
- Lehman Brothers – $183 billion
- Bank of Scotland – $181 billion
- BNP Paribas – $175 billion
- Wells Fargo – $159 billion
- Dexia – $159 billion
- Wachovia – $142 billion
- Dresdner Bank – $135 billion
- Societe Generale – $124 billion
- "All Other Borrowers" – $2.639 trillion

This report was made available to all the members of Congress, but most of them have been silent about it. One of the only members of Congress that have said something has been U.S. Senator Bernie Sanders.

Not only did the Federal Reserve give 16.1 trillion dollars in nearly interest-free loans to the "too big to fail" banks, but the Fed also paid them over 600 million dollars to help run the emergency lending program. According to the GAO, the Federal Reserve shelled out an astounding $659.4 million in "fees" to the very financial institutions which caused the financial crisis in the first place.

Besides, it turns out that trillions of dollars of this bailout money went overseas. According to the GAO audit, approximately $3.08 trillion went to foreign banks in Europe and Asia.

It's important to understand that many of these bailout loans were made at below market interest rates, and this enabled many of these financial institutions to rake in huge profits. According to a Bloomberg article, the big banks brought in an estimated $13 billion by taking advantage of the Fed's below-market rates.

By now this bailout strategy is standard for most industrial countries in the world. Europa and other countries are following the U.S. with massive bailouts. Broke nations are bailing out other broke countries with borrowed money.

Sometimes they are called "bailouts" and sometimes they are called other things, but in every single case, they involve loans. Also, most of the time, these loans come with very stringent conditions. It is a form of "global governance" most people don't know.

For decades, the IMF (International Monetary Fund) has been able to use money as a way to force developing nations to do what it wants them to do. However, up until relatively recently, this had in most cases only be done with developing nations. Now an increasing number of wealthy nations are turning to the IMF for help.

The IMF is funded by "wealthy" nations that dominate the global economy. Its hidden purpose is to enslave countries and nations. This starts with the promise of cheap loans to help these nations to increase their prosperity. Once the loans have been provided to these nations, they are on the hook for the yearly interest payment. If these payments are difficult to make, the IMF is happy to negotiate but demand control over resources and political power. The whole process starts very smoothly in the beginning, but over time countries and entire nations are sold out and enslaved.

Where does the IMF get their money? Hard to believe, but they are getting it from a bunch of nations that are drowning in debt themselves.

The following is how Wikipedia describes the IMF's quota system: „The IMF's quota system was created to raise funds for loans. Each IMF member country is assigned a quota, or contribution, that reflects the country's relative size in the global economy. Each member's quota also determines its relative voting power. Thus, financial contributions from member governments are linked to voting power in the organization."

These are the five largest contributors to IMF funding:

- United States – 16.75%
- Japan – 6.23%
- Germany – 5.81%
- France – 4.29%
- UK – 4.29%

However, those countries are in trouble themselves. The U.S. has a debt to GDP ratio of over 100%. Japan has a debt to GDP ratio of over 200%. The truth is that these countries are funding the IMF with borrowed money.

All over the globe, an increasing number of countries are reaching out to the IMF for help. Once a nation gets hooked on bailout money from the IMF or other international sources, it can be tough to get off of it.

However, that is the real intention of these globalist organizations. They want to be able to use money as a form of control.

What happens when the nations that primarily fund the IMF start failing themselves? The U.S. is a complete and total financial disaster, and so is Japan. Much of Europe was already experiencing a full-blown economic depression, and now even China is showing signs of trouble.

Keep in mind that every bailout is nothing more than a loan with interest. The loan and interest have to be paid back. In most cases it's impossible for a country to pay back the loan, because it does not have the money and would need to declare bankruptcy. Besides that, all currency in circulation is debt (borrowed currency) - therefore banks are not interested that loans are being paid back. They make their profit on the interest, as long as the loan is outstanding!

The moment a loan is renewed or extended the interest has to be paid. Guess where this additional money for the interest payment comes from? Yes, from you of course - in the form of additional taxes and fees!

Robbing Method #7 - Debasing the Currency

"Give me control of a nation's money and I care not who makes the laws."- Mayer Amschel Rothschild, Banker and the founder of the Rothschild banking dynasty

To finance the expansion of the Roman empire, a massive military force was established. The Roman empire was fighting wars in all directions, and the expenses skyrocket. Debasing the money was a temporary way to finance it, but eventually, it caused the collapse of one of the most powerful and wealthy empires the world has ever seen.

Chris Horlacher points out that for hundreds of years, the Romans were on a bimetallic standard, not unlike the currency system of the early United States. There was a gold coin, the aureus, which was popularized by Julius Caesar. There was also a silver coin known as the denarius, which was what most Romans used in their day to day transactions. It was on a solid gold and silver standard that Rome ascended to the height of its development and power.

When Julius Caesar first began minting large quantities of the aureus, it was 8 grams of pure gold. By the second century it had declined to 6.5 grams, and at the beginning of the fourth century, it was replaced by the 4.5-gram solidus. The purity of the coin itself was never debased, but the ever decreasing weight was a sure sign that government spending had been outpacing revenues for centuries.

All of this pales in comparison with the devaluation of the denarius. The denarius was the backbone of the Roman economy. Citizens earning their income in gold were a rarity given that a day's wage for an average laborer at the time is estimated at a single denarius. Thus it also became the target of severe abuse by the Roman authorities.

The denarius began as a 4.5-gram silver coin and had stayed that way for centuries under the Roman Republic. After Rome became an empire, things started to turn sour for the denarius and, by extension, the Roman economy. Base metals, such as copper were blended in with the silver and so even though the coin itself weighed the same, the amount of silver in it became less and less with each successive emperor. Throughout the first century the denarius contained over 90% silver, but by the end of the second century, the silver content had fallen to less than 70%. A century later there was less than 5% silver in the coin, and by 350 AD it was all but worthless, having an exchange rate of 4,600,000 to a gold solidus (or nearly 9 million to the original aureus).

The economic chaos, the hyperinflation of the denarius had on Roman society, was genuine. The population of Rome reached a peak of about 1 million inhabitants during the first century BC and maintained that level until nearly the end of the second century. At this point, it began to decline throughout the third century slowly and precipitously throughout the fourth. By the fifth century, only about 50 thousand people remained.

Various measures were introduced until today to stop clipping. Machines that make the coins are milling (ridges) around the edge of the coin. Even today as coins do not contain any precious metals you still see the ridges on it.[11]

Reasons that a government chooses to debase the currency in this way center around the financial benefits that the government can reap. Governments that lowered the quantity of gold and silver in their coinage found that they could quietly mint more coins from a fixed amount of metal on hand.

The downside to this for the general population centers on the inflation that this in turn causes. Such inflation is yet another benefit for the currency debasing government that then finds that it can pay off government debt or repudiate government bonds easier. The populace's purchasing power is significantly reduced as a result of this, along with their then lowered standard of living.

Debasing a currency lowers the value of the currency in question. Given enough time and abuse by the governing authorities, this debasing can even lead to a collapse in the existing currency that causes a newer currency or coinage to be created and launched for the nation or state.

Competitive devaluation is a condition in international affairs, where countries seek to gain a trade advantage over other nations by causing the exchange rate of their currency to fall in relation to other currencies. As the exchange rate of a country's currency falls exports become more competitive in other countries, and imports into the country become more expensive. Both effects benefit the domestic industry, and thus employment, which receives a boost in demand from both domestic and foreign markets. However, the price increases for import goods (as well as in the cost of foreign travel) are unpopular as they harm citizens' purchasing power.

When all countries adopt a similar strategy, which by now they do, it will lead to a general decline in international trade, harming all countries. It will also be the underlining cause of civil unrest.

Anyone who has paid but the briefest attention to the critics of such methods will know, the risk to such financial magic is the devastating consequences of too-high inflation. Imports will immediately become more expensive, as will commodity prices in local terms. Simply put, you will have to pay more for what you buy.[12]

Robbing Method #8 - Derivatives

"In our view, however, derivatives are financial weapons of mass destruction, carrying dangers that, while now latent, are potentially lethal." - Warren Buffett, American business magnate & investor

Financial products known as derivatives are at the heart of what explains the now out-of-control growth of finance in stagnant economic times. The Bank for International Settlements estimates the total amount of outstanding derivative products to be $647.8 trillion. That compares with an estimate (nominal) of total world GDP of $69.6 trillion by the IMF. Thus, measured as the amount of notional financial claims - we owe you, you owe us - the stock of derivatives is over nine times greater than the market value of goods and services produced around the world in one year.[13]

The derivatives story began in earnest when the fixed foreign exchange rates era ended in the early 1970s. Banks started to trade currencies the way commodities had been traded, as "futures." Instead of selling U.S. dollars today and taking a commission for the trade, banks would sell you a promise to deliver U.S. dollars in six months or a year, and charge you a fee.

Derivatives Are Bets

Duncan Cameron explains that in essence, a financial derivative is a contract that entitles the holder to a claim on an asset. It is not the asset itself. It is the right to buy or sell the asset. Banks created the markets for financial derivatives and took fees from buyers and sellers alike. The business of finance came to revolve around making demands in new forms of derivatives.

Beginning with commodities, and currencies, derivatives trading expanded to include interest rates, equities and credit derivatives, including the infamous credit default swaps and collateralized debt obligations or CDOs, that led to the financial collapse of 2008 and required the bailouts of major banks around the world by national governments.

Any person holding an asset, be it funds in a bank account, a residence, a painting, or a stock portfolio has established a "long" position favoring that asset. There is no obvious need to "hedge" each long position by artificially creating a "short" position, in effect betting banks will fail, mortgages will default, a painter go out of fashion, or stock collapse. That mentality is what credit derivatives trades feed upon, and what substantial hedge funds exploit.

One of the causes of the 2008 financial crisis was the proliferation of unregulated derivatives in the last decade. An excellent example of a derivative is a mortgage-backed security. Most derivatives start with a real asset. Here's how they work, using mortgage-backed security as an example.[14]

- A bank lends money to a homebuyer.

- The bank then sells the mortgage to Fannie Mae. This gives the bank more funds to make new loans.

- Fannie Mae resells the mortgage in a package of other mortgages on the secondary market. This is a mortgage-backed security, which has a value that is derived from the value of the mortgages in the bundle.

- Often the MBS (Mortgage-Backed Security) is bought by a hedge fund, which then slices out a portion of the MBS, let's say the second and third years of the interest-only loans, which is riskier since it is farther out, but also provides a higher interest payment. It uses sophisticated computer programs to figure out all this complexity. It then combines it with similar risk levels of other MBS and resells just that portion, called a tranche, to additional hedge funds.

- All goes well until housing prices decline or interest rates reset, and the mortgages start to default.

Before the financial crisis of 2008, many of the borrowers had interest-only loans, which are a type of adjustable-rate mortgage. Unlike a conventional loan, the interest rates rises along with the fed funds rate. When the Federal Reserve started raising rates, these mortgage-holders found they could no longer afford the payments. It happened at the same time the interest rates reset - usually after three years.

As the interest rates rose, demand for housing fell, and so did home prices. These mortgage-holders found they couldn't make the payments or sell the house, so they started defaulting.

Most important, some parts of the MBS were worthless, but no one could figure out which parts. Since no one understood what was in the MBS, no one knew what the actual value of the MBS was. This uncertainty led to a shut-down of the secondary market, which now meant that the banks and hedge funds had lots of derivatives that were both declining in value and that they couldn't sell.

Soon, banks stopped lending to each other altogether, because they were afraid of receiving more defaulting derivatives as collateral. When this happened, they started hoarding cash to pay for their day-to-day operations.

That is what prompted the bank bailout bill. It was initially designed to get these derivatives off of the books of banks so they can start making loans again.

It is not just mortgages that provide the underlying value for derivatives. Other types of loans and assets can, too. For example, if the underlying value is corporate debt, credit card debt or auto loans, then the derivative is called a collateralized debt obligation.

If you find this explanation too complicated, here is a short story that illustrates this context may be better.

The Story of Heidi's Drink Bonds

Heidi is the owner of a bar in Detroit. She realizes that almost all of her customers are unemployed and, as such, can no longer afford to visit her bar.

To solve this problem, she comes up with a new marketing plan that allows her customers to drink now, but pay later. Heidi keeps track of the drinks consumed on a ledger (thereby granting the customers loans).

Word gets around about Heidi's "drink now, pay later" marketing strategy and, as a result, increasing numbers of customers flood into Heidi's bar. Soon she has the largest sales volume for any bar in Detroit.

By providing her customers freedom from immediate payment demands, Heidi gets no resistance when, at regular intervals, she substantially increases her prices for wine and beer, the most consumed beverages. Consequently, Heidi's gross sales volume increases massively.

A young and dynamic vice-president at Heidi's local bank recognizes these customer debts constitute valuable future assets and increases Heidi's borrowing limit. He sees no reason for any undue concern since he has the obligations of the unemployed alcoholics as collateral!

At the bank's corporate headquarters, expert traders figure out a way to make huge commissions and transform these customer loans into DRINK BONDS. These "securities" are bundled and traded on international securities markets. Naive investors don't understand the securities being sold to them as "AAA Secured Bonds" really are debts of unemployed alcoholics.

Nevertheless, the bond prices continuously climb, and the securities soon become the hottest-selling items for some of the nation's leading brokerage houses.

One day, even though the bond prices still are climbing, a risk manager at the original local bank decides that the time has come to demand payment on the debts incurred by Heidi's bar. He informs Heidi. Heidi then requires payment from her alcoholic patrons, but being unemployed alcoholics; they cannot pay back their drinking debts.

Since Heidi cannot fulfill her loan obligations to the bank, she is forced into bankruptcy. The bar closes, and Heidi's 11 employees lose their jobs. Overnight, DRINK BOND prices drop by 90%.

The collapsed bond asset value destroys the bank's liquidity and prevents it from issuing new loans, thus freezing credit and economic activity in the community. The suppliers of Heidi's bar had granted her generous payment extensions and had invested their firms' pension funds in the bond securities. They find out; they are now faced with writing off her bad debt and losing over 90% of the presumed value of the bonds.

Her wine supplier also claims bankruptcy, closing the doors on a family business that had endured for three generations, her beer supplier is taken over by a competitor, who immediately closes the local plant and lays off 150 workers. Besides, the laid-off workers' pension funds and Individual Retirement Accounts all suffer a substantial loss in value.

Fortunately, though, the bank, brokerage houses and their respective executives are saved and bailed out by a multi-billion dollar, no-strings attached cash infusion from the government.

The funds required for this bailout are obtained by new taxes levied on employed, middle-class nondrinkers who have never been in or heard of Heidi's bar.

Robbing Method #9 - Special Drawing Rights (SDR)

„The issuing power [of money] should be taken from the banks and restored to the people, to whom it properly belongs." - Thomas Jefferson, American Founding Father

Whenever you use a credit card or send a bank transfer, you're using a digital form of currency. This concept dates back to the Middle Ages when Italian bankers realized that they could conduct their transactions without physical money. Rather than risk transporting gold coins across the countryside, medieval bankers merely annotated their ledgers with debit and credit entries. They didn't have the computers, but it was the same concept – they kept track of transactions and balances on account ledgers, instead of with physical money.[15]

In the late 1960s, the IMF took this idea to the next level when they created their own digital currency for the exclusive use of governments and central banks. They're called Special Drawing Rights (SDR, or XDR). Even though the IMF's balance sheet totals nearly 475 billion SDR (around $645 billion) as of March 2017, not a single SDR exists in physical form.

100% of the SDR money supply is digital. Just like Bitcoin, it exists in computer databases, making it the digital equivalent of a 500-year old accounting system.

Boiled down to its essence, the SDR is a kind of super money printed by the IMF.

Since Federal Reserve resources were barely able to prevent the complete collapse in 2008, it should be expected that an even more massive collapse will overwhelm the Fed's balance sheet.

Jim Rickards mentioned in his books the SDR, and he is one of the leading financial analysts in the US. He said that next time, printing another $3 trillion-plus won't be politically feasible. "The specter of the sovereign debt crisis suggests the urgency for new liquidity sources, bigger than those that central banks can provide, the next time a liquidity crisis strikes. The logic leads quickly from one world to one bank to one currency for the planet."

Leading the way, says Rickards, will be the International Monetary Fund. "The task of re-liquefying the world will fall to the IMF, because the IMF will have the only clean balance sheet left among official institutions. The IMF will rise to the occasion with a towering issuance of SDRs, and this monetary operation will effectively end the dollar's role as the leading reserve currency."

The name is cryptic. The mechanism will prove far more inscrutable than the Fed's alphabet-soup bailout programs in 2008. However, the objective will be the same - to print money in the interest of keeping a rotten system functioning.

Typically, SDR's are used to take loans or make repayments made by the IMF. They are also used by its members' central banks to sell to help currency reserves during times of economic crisis.[16]

SDR's are Banks' Super Money

Boiled down to its essence, the SDR is a kind of super money printed by the IMF and then circulated among central banks and governments. Indeed, the IMF has issued SDRs three times since their creation more than 40 years ago. Each time it was linked to a crisis of confidence in the U.S. dollar.

In fact, it enhances that role by making the SDR invisible to citizens. The SDR can be issued in abundance to IMF members and can also be used in the future for a select list of the most important transactions in the world, including balance-of-payments settlements, oil pricing and the financial accounts of the world's largest corporations, such as Exxon Mobil, Toyota and Royal Dutch Shell.

The genius of the scheme is that the SDRs would create inflation, but ordinary people wouldn't know SDRs were causing it. "Any inflation caused by massive SDR issuance would not be immediately apparent to citizens. The inflation would show up eventually in dollars, yen, and euros at the gas pump or the grocery, but national central banks could deny responsibility with ease and point the finger at the IMF."

"A financial panic in the next several years, caused by derivatives exposure and bank interconnectedness, may trigger a global liquidity crisis worse than the 1998 and 2008 crises," he writes in his book. The IMF will step in but "the emerging circumstances will mean the process will be carried out on a crash basis, without reference to carefully constructed infrastructure now contemplated."

The IMF member states have exclusive membership to this currency club, and only four countries are in that group "basket" – for now. It means that the IMF weighs all of the member currency values into a standard rate which changes daily.

Currently, the U.S dollar, European Union euro, Japanese yen, and U.K pound sterling make up the SDR. As of midnight on September 30, China's renminbi will join the elite club. Membership has only changed once in the past three decades.

The IMF is the only institution that can print and distribute world money. Only its member states that are within its elite "basket" can freely exchange SDR as currency.

Robbing Method #10 - Silver & Gold Leasing

"A business that makes nothing but money is a poor business."
– Henry Ford

By now you know that silver and gold were once used as money and that we currently use fiat money: money that has no intrinsic value that a government has declared as legal tender. Fiat money, like the US dollar, is based on faith. It only has value if everyone in the nation believes they can exchange it for goods and services. Conversely, gold and silver have physical and utility value; they look nice, are nice to have when displaying wealth, and can be used for industrial purposes. For those who disagree with their use in industrial applications, consider that there is gold in every cell phone and half of the silver demand is industrial.[17]

The faith in a nation's fiat currency is tested when a government overprints it, relative to economic output, and the value of the fiat money declines. This is also known as inflation and is seen as a general rise in prices. When this happens, citizens and investors start looking at substitutes to the fiat money that is declining in value.

Silver and gold are substitute stores of value and become attractive when a fiat currency depreciates. This is why silver and gold are threats to governments that issue fiat currencies; they can't control silver and gold like they can their fiat money, and they don't want to lose the power that comes with control over their currencies. Thus, governments have a reason to reduce the appeal of silver and gold and discourage their purchases. One way to do that is to keep them underpriced by leasing it out.

This phenomenon is called the silver & gold leasing scam. After years of turning a blind eye to it, the Commodities and Futures Trading Commission has finally opened an exhaustive investigation into the practice.

The effects of this investigation are wide-ranging and could dramatically impact the market prices for silver in the near to medium term future.

What is the Purpose of Leasing Silver & Gold?

Why would someone want to lease out his or her silver & gold in the first place? The mega-banks hold vast inventories of silver and gold to back up their financial institutions and reassure depositors and customers that they are stable. These precious metals preserve the long-term wealth of the bank quite well. The problem that these bullion banks have with their vast holdings, is that they do not generate any wealth when they sit in the vaults and collect dust.

Greed entered the picture as the big bullion banks looked for a way to earn some revenue from these silver and gold holdings. They did not want to sell their precious silver stockpiles, but only to find a way to make income on them while they are on the balance sheet. The answer to this dilemma that the bullion banks faced was to lease out the metals. If they could find some smaller banks to loan the metals to at the rate of one to two percent of the actual silver metal value each year, then they would be able to realize revenues and profits while they still maintained legal ownership of the precious metals.

How Can Silver & Gold be Leased?

It is easy to see how the major banks were able to lease out their silver & gold, once they found willing customers. They would sign a contract for a period and charge an interest rate. Then they would deliver the physical silver & gold to a customer with the understanding that they did not have to receive the same silver & gold back. This is what makes silver leasing possible. So long as they get the exact weight of the silver &

gold bars back at the end of their lease, the primary institution that owns the silver & gold is perfectly happy.

The willing customers that the mega-banks found to lease their silver & gold turned out to be smaller banks that also had an idea to make money from the silver & gold lease. These small banks were willing to pay a one to two percent fee for the use of the precious metals because they would turn around and sell this silver on the open market. They could then take the money that they received and invest it into stable assets with a higher yield of three to four percent, such as Treasuries or other safe investments. This gave them the income to pay their lease fees and still make a percent or two for themselves.

The main problem with silver & gold leasing is the creation of a false scenario in the market. Most banks that do these leases never intend to return the metal. They keep rolling their lease contracts over with the large bullion banks.

Since the small banks that lease the silver & gold from the silver & gold owning banks turn around and sell the metal without any plans to re-purchase and return it, it makes it look like there is far more silver & gold on the world market than there really is. The additional supply that has been sold does not exist since it has been borrowed. Although the supply is a lie and unreal, the depressing effect that it has on the prices is real. An appearance of too much supply serves to keep the prices of silver & gold artificially low.

Who is Behind the Leasing Scam?

By this point, you probably wondering who could be involved in such unscrupulous activity as to loan out silver & gold that they never intend to repatriate while they still show it on their balance sheet as inventory on hand. The Commodities and Futures Trading Commission's ongoing investigation has helped to make it possible to name culprits and point fingers of blame. JP Morgan is considered to be one of the worst offenders for leasing out silver, but it is not alone. Goldman Sachs, HSBC, AIG, and the Bank of Nova Scotia are others whose names are on the list of habitual offenders.

Since an investigation is already underway, the silver & gold leasing scam is currently in the process of being exposed.

In 2016 Deutsche Bank AG has agreed to pay $60 million to settle private U.S. antitrust litigation by traders and other investors who accused the German bank of conspiring to manipulate gold prices at their expense.

The longer-term ramifications of the end of the silver & gold lease practices are more significant than this. Should the point come where the activity is declared illegal and broken up, the banks that borrowed the silver & gold do not have it, and will not be able to return it. This is mainly a problem because there is so little inventory of physical silver available for them to buy and return. In fact, there is an insufficient quantity of silver above ground for them to make good on their borrowed silver commitments.

To put it in perspective, an entire two years of silver production has been loaned out and sold for such industrial applications as medical products, electrical and computer goods, solar panels, military hardware, photography, and thousands of other applications. This silver has been used up and cannot be recovered.

Meanwhile, there is not even an entire year's worth of silver supply available above ground to be purchased. You can see that silver prices would have to go far higher for the borrowing banks to have any hope at all of returning their sliver lease metals. On top of all this, it's possible that they would not be able to obtain this quantity of silver today at any price.

Besides potentially much higher silver prices and even silver shortages, there will likely be legal consequences when silver & gold leasing is prohibited. There is already speculation that the firms from JP Morgan and Goldman Sachs to AIG and Bank of Nova Scotia that have engaged in it will be held liable and charged enormous civil and regulatory penalties since they will have been found guilty of silver manipulation that went on for over fifteen years. It is highly possible that the principals of these companies, who made the decisions to lease out the silver illegally, will also face criminal prosecution and even substantial time in prison.

Robbing Method #11 - The Education System

"Education would be much more effective if its purpose was to ensure that by the time they leave school every boy and girl should know how much they do not know, and be imbued with a lifelong desire to know it." - William Haley, British editor & director BBC

With the beginning of this chapter, we will discuss the more subtle and psychological ways of robbing your money. These methods are not as apparent as - for example - taxes, but they are even more devastating because you are mostly unaware of them.

Who wants to start its career with $50,00 - $100,000 in debt? To make you pay for education almost guarantees to create more thieves and bank robbers and homeless people.

To charge for education is a crime by itself. It forces and encourages people to fall into their dark side. It brings out the worst in people instead of cultivating the good. If you are in debt when you start your career, your choices are limited to job opportunities that guarantee you when and how to pay back your loan. It's a perfect setup that ensures that you end up exactly where the banks and the government want you to be.

A job is something you are seeking outside of yourself. It's a deliberately promoted mindset, which includes the belief that there is a limited amount of possibilities 'out' there, where you can make money. It's the assumption that there specific categories, where you have to fit in. It is the assumption that you have to match one of those limited categories with who you are. It's a tough task - if not impossible - and it will get even more difficult in the future through automation.

It all starts in early childhood with the question: "What do you want to be when you are a grown up?" It already implies that you can't stay or be who you are - with your intrinsic values, gifts, and talents that have been given to you from day one since birth. You are forced to become someone else. You have to leave your artistic heritage behind and learn to become someone else that fits the profile of the economic structure. It reminds me of a saying: „Be yourself, everybody else is already taken."

By the way when did we start using the name job instead of work?

The dictionaries first explanation is: „a piece of work, especially a specific task done as part of the routine of one's occupation or for an agreed price."

As you can see from the definition, jobs have the intrinsic meaning that they are temporary. It has become nothing less than a task. Work that was used to be a life's assignment in the past is now split into short-term economic snippets. It has become a soulless, meaningless transaction - your time in exchange for money. That's where the phrase 'time is money' originates and this all started with the industrial revolution.

The Current School System

The current school system was set up in the late 1800s and early 1900s, to meet the needs of the industrial economy.

Public schools supplied factories with a skilled labor force and provided basic literacy to the masses. It was the education that the vast majority of the population received.

Secondary education supplied the managerial and professional leadership of the industrial economy. It provided more flexible and widely applicable skills that could be transferred across firms, industries, and occupations.

Higher education supplied the engineers, doctors, and scientists which facilitated rapid urbanization and technological advancement for the economy. Still, less than 5% of the population attained this level of education by the 1940s.

The school system was modeled after the factories of the industrial revolution. Schools and factories are similar even to the point where the bells at these schools were modeled on the shift-time sounds in factories.[18]

Schools operate similarly to assembly lines. The school assembly line is segmented into years, students enter it and are sorted by age. Each day during the year students receive instructions on particular subjects and skill sets. Every subject is taught during a fixed time in the day. Students are then tested on each topic to see if they meet the standards so that they can move along the line. Finally, they receive their stamp of approval (diploma) at the end of the line.

One Mold Fits All

The schools believed in a model of education where one mold fitted everybody and turned to learn into a dull, repetitive, and tedious process. Our school system provided training for a large segment of the population that did not have the resources to be educated in any other way.

There was also a sound rationale for children to want to go to school. Public schools effectively provided the skills necessary to succeed in the industrial economy. Public school graduates could expect to find a job with relative ease and have job security for the rest of their lives.

Today we live in a post-industrial economy and a rapidly globalizing world. The job security that previous generations enjoyed no longer exists.

Today a person changes jobs every three years on average.

We can hardly anticipate what the economy would look like in a month, or what set of skills it would require. Our industrial age school system cannot keep up with such rapid changes.

Schools have become a significant burden, without much benefit. Going through the system can no longer guarantee success in the 21st century. A person who chooses to rely on the skill set he acquired at school may quickly discover that his skills are obsolete.

Reforms Made it Even Worth

So what have our leaders and government done to address the issues at the core of the problem? States established higher education standards. Student performance was measured more rigorously, requiring more student testing and holding educators responsible for the results.

Because teachers' jobs depend on their students passing the test, they focused on teaching what will be on the test, instead of focusing on making the students proficient on the subject. The results show that students are passing the criteria, but are not competent in the subjects.

In other words, the school became more rigorous and mechanical, but the scope or quality of education did not improve, and the assembly line model of education remained the same. School no longer serves to expand students' possibilities in life, or enrich their experience. Instead, it focuses on passing meaningless standardized tests.

Many students are being forced to conform to a mold that does not fit them, and they see no benefit in doing so. They are told to pay attention to subjects that do not interest them, and that is taught dully and tediously. As a result, students retain very little of what they're taught. The only thing students are taught in schools is to hate education.

Students are mistrusted by the school system and are viewed as immature and irresponsible. In some schools, students are routinely searched for weapons. The schools demand respect for authority from the students and decry the lack of discipline in classes.

The natural response of many students is to resist the conditions they are being subjected. Instead of engaging the students, students are being disciplined and penalized. When they are bored in class, they are told that they're inadequate. That they have a medical disorder because they can't pay attention, and are prescribed powerful drugs to make them docile. Because they only know that it's not working for them, and they do not know of anything better, they resist and become depressed. Their only power left is to boycott the system and instead do nothing.

Who could blame them?

Suppressing Creativity - Creating Uniformity

Because of its industrial roots, our school system considers some subjects (math, reading, and science) to be useful and vital, while others (music, art, drama) useless and unimportant. While the former subjects indeed are essential, the latter is no less critical.

While math and science require accuracy and precision, the arts promote divergent thinking and creativity. Our economy thrives on creativity and innovation, yet our schools systematically suppress these qualities.

Even in the subjects that are considered essential, students' performance is only superficially assessed by standardized testing. It means that instead of putting effort into making the topic interesting and engaging to students, educators can rely on teaching dully and tediously to achieve an acceptable result.

In a Nutshell

The current school system confuses the students, one sees and hears something, only to forget it again. It teaches to accept class affiliation, makes them indifferent, emotionally and intellectually dependent. It educates an illusionary self-confidence, which requires the constant confirmation by experts to keep this false illusionary self-confidence alive.

It lays the early foundation of a competing attitude, which leads to stress, rapid exhaustion and later adulthood that is driven by fear and scarcity. Being already in debt takes the rest of the soul into the graveyard.

Topics and methods that are thought are entirely outdated and provide skills for jobs that won't exist any longer after school is finished. It is based on an old model that was fitting the job requirements of the industrial revolution.

If you have a job - don't do it for the sake of money. Do it, because you want to learn what there is to learn from it. When there is nothing more to gain - move on. If you do the job only for the money, you are stuck forever in the ,rat race', and you don't evolve.

Robbing Method #12 - The Insurance Scam

„Life insurance is a policy that keeps you poor all your life so that you can die rich." - Author Unknown

People buy products for two reasons. Either to get things they want or to avoid the things they don't want. Fear industries focus on the latter. Something is going to go wrong. We will rescue you from financial catastrophe.

The insurance business is probably one of the few industries that have managed to institutionalize the concept of selling fear successfully; fear of a scary tomorrow. A market where consumers pay money upfront for a service or benefit that they may never need.[19]

They are cleverly tricking your mind to go from the present moment, where everything is fine, into the future. Insurance companies take you there with a simple question - like this one: „What would happen to your family if you got a serious illness and you are no longer able to work?" If you are falling into that mind trap, your mind assumes for a moment that this scenario is real. You will instantly feel you have lost control over your life.

Fear disconnects you from who you are and your responsibility!

If you still think at this point some insurances are necessary, then that's an indication of how strong that belief is embedded in your mind. Insurance people are professionals in manipulating your thinking, so it works against you and for them. Insurance companies are not interested in helping you, they are a business, and the goal is to make a profit from you.

There is a now-famous experiment, that was done by two researchers, Amos Tversky and Daniel Kahneman. They examined how people make decisions involving risk. The work was done in an area of research known as behavioral finance, and the results can be extrapolated to any purchase that involves a risk. The conclusion was that people are willing to run higher risks to avoid losses than they are to make gains.

In the early days of human societies, also called natural or non-monetary economies, people used barter and trade. Insurance entailed an agreement of mutual aid. If one family's house gets destroyed, the neighbors were committed to helping rebuild it. One of the strategies of a modern centralized monetary system is to isolate people from each other. To instill a belief that they are more in control and better off on themselves. This principle leads to the accumulation of products that now belongs to only one person, which could have been shared between people.

You can see what's happening by just scanning through this list of different insurances. That list is far from complete, but it's long enough to get the point across.

- Aviation insurance
- Bancassurance
- Boiler insurance
- Bond insurance
- Builder's risk insurance
- Business interruption insurance
- Business overhead expense disability insurance
- Casualty insurance
- Catastrophe bond
- Chargeback insurance
- Collateral protection insurance
- Computer insurance
- Condo insurance
- Contents insurance
- Credit insurance
- Critical illness insurance
- Cyber-Insurance

- Death bond
- Dental insurance
- Deposit insurance
- Directors and officers liability insurance
- Divorce insurance
- Dual trigger insurance
- Earthquake insurance
- Expatriate insurance
- Extended warranties
- Flight accident insurance
- Fidelity bond
- Financial reinsurance
- Flood insurance
- GAP insurance
- General insurance
- Group insurance
- Guaranteed asset protection insurance

- Health insurance
- Home insurance
- Income protection insurance
- Inland marine insurance
- Identity theft insurance
- Interest rate insurance
- Key person insurance
- Kidnap and ransom insurance
- Life insurance
- Labor insurance (Japan)
- Landlords' insurance
- Legal expenses insurance
- Liability insurance
- Longevity insurance
- Microinsurance
- Multiple-peril insurance
- Mutual insurance
- Niche Insurance
- No-fault insurance
- Over-redemption insurance
- Owner-controlled insurance program
- Parametric insurance
- Payment protection insurance
- Pension insurance contract
- Pension term assurance
- Perpetual insurance
- Pet insurance
- Political risk insurance
- Pollution insurance
- Prize indemnity insurance
- Property insurance
- Rent guarantee insurance
- Renters' insurance
- Retrospectively rated insurance
- Satellite insurance
- Shipping insurance
- Stop-loss insurance
- Tenancy Deposit Scheme (England and Wales)
- Tenancy deposit schemes (Scotland)
- Terminal illness insurance
- Terrorism insurance
- Total permanent disability insurance
- Trade credit insurance
- Travel insurance
- Tuition insurance
- Vehicle insurance
- Wage insurance
- War risk insurance
- Weather insurance
- Worker's compensation (Germany)
- Workers' accident compensation insurance (Japan)
- Workers' compensation
- Workers' compensation employer defense

Because this isolation technique worked so well, most people are now left alone if anything happens to them. Another reason for having insurance is the number of products that now come with astronomical prices. Most people could never afford a car that costs $20.000 or $30.000. They either have to lease it or make payments to the bank. If you crash that car, you are most likely financially broke. That's where the insurance comes in.

Even worse are housing prices now. They have become so expensive that many people can't pay them off in a lifetime. You need insurance for flood and hurricane, and on top, you need protection if you can't pay the mortgage any longer. It's just a debt spiral that ends in the abyss.

The last time I went into an office store and bought a chair, the cashier asked me if I wanted insurance for that chair. I said: "Insurance? Why?" The man looked at me and said: „Because it may last only 1-2 years".

How much money does your health insurance cost you? How much is that in a percentage of your income? The only point of your health insurance is that you stay in the rat race. When you are sick doctors are not interested in curing you - they can't! They will prescribe you something that helps with your symptoms. They will patch you up so you could quickly go back to work. However, that will not address why you got sick in the first place and over time things will get worse.

Medical insurance is what allows people to be ill at ease.

As mentioned before, because of inflation, most people can no longer afford basic stuff like cars, furniture, houses, education and so on. That's why most of these products have to be sold with financing, and most financing requires insurance. Financing lures you into the belief that you can afford the product, but in reality, you can't. Because of massive inflation of the currency people get poorer every year, and wages hardly increase - in most cases, they are stuck for years if not decades.

Robbing Method #13 - Perpetual Consumption

„The so-called consumer society and the politics of corporate capitalism have created a second nature of man which ties him libidinally and aggressively to the commodity form. The need for possessing, consuming, handling and constantly renewing the gadgets, devices, instruments, engines, offered to and imposed upon the people, for using these wares even at the danger of one's own destruction, has become a ‚biological' need." - Herbert Marcuse, German-American philosopher, sociologist, and political theorist

Perpetual is defined as never-ending or changing. It has become one of the main bloodstreams of an industrial nation. Let's recap. For a government to pay back the interest on the loan from the bank, the government needs to figure out a way to create an annual growth rate that matches the interest payment.

A never ending growth cycle means the following:

- Higher prices for goods and services
- More products
- More sick people
- More government spending
- More trash
- More industries
- More pollution
- More weapons and defense systems
- Less freedom
- Less nature

Even if the growth rate is only 2% per year, the time it takes to use up all resources and to make the planet inhabitable is extremely short. Because we are dealing with percentage, the growth happens in a logarithmic way. In the beginning, the increase is unnoticeable for a long time, however, toward the end, the growth occurs so fast that it becomes almost unstoppable. Let me give you a short primer on logarithmic growth to demonstrate this.

The Overlooked Power of Logarithmic Growth

There's a famous legend about the origin of chess. When the inventor of the game showed it to the emperor of India, the emperor was so impressed by the new game, that he said to the man: "Name your reward!"

The man responded, "Oh emperor, my wishes are simple. I only wish for this. Give me one grain of rice for the first square of the chessboard, two grains for the next square, four for the next, eight for the next and so on for all 64 squares, with each square having double the number of grains as the square before."

The emperor agreed, amazed that the man had asked for such a small reward - or so he thought. After a week, his treasurer came back and informed him that the reward would add up to an astronomical sum, far higher than all the rice that could conceivably be produced in many many centuries!

Exponential growth is extremely powerful. One of the most critical features of exponential growth is that, while it starts off slowly, it can result in enormous quantities reasonably quickly - often in a way that is shocking.

Exponential growth occurs when a quantity grows by the same relative amount - that is, by the same percentage - in each unit of time. Linear growth occurs when a quantity increases by the same absolute amount in each unit of time.

If the population of ants increases by 1,000 every month, it grows with linear growth. If the population of ants increases by 20% every month, it improves with exponential growth.

When most people talk about 'growth,' they consider it a positive and necessary thing, essential for maintaining the vitality and health of our economy and society.

Our society's most revered economic indicators are all based on this fundamental idea: that continuing growth is vital for the health and preservation of our economy and country. In fact, growth is pretty much the only thing they measure!

However, natural scientists (such as biologists, chemists, and physicists) know that this assumption must be false. For growth to continue forever, we would need an infinite amount of space, energy, and other resources to keep the growth going. Most of the resources we're using right now are not infinite.

What happens to steady growth in a limited space? To help explain, we're going to use a simple example of bacteria growing in a bottle.

The Bacteria Growing Example

Let's assume the bacteria have all the food they need. In this story, the only limits to the bacteria's growth are the walls of their bottle.[20]

At 11:00, we place a single bacterium in a bottle. It's so small you'd need a microscope to see it! In one minute it grows to twice its original size and divides in half, reproducing itself, so at 11:01 there are two bacteria in the bottle.

The bacteria continue to grow and to divide, doubling their numbers every minute, so by 11:02 there are four, and by 11:03 there are eight. At the end of five minutes, there are 32 bacteria where there used to be just one. They're still so small; they can't be seen without a microscope.

The bacteria keep doubling their numbers every minute, until 12:00, when the bottle fills up. When do you suppose the bottle was half full?

At 11:59, the bottle is half full! Since the bottle filled up at 12:00, it must have been half full just a minute before.

At 11:45 we could barely see the bacteria, and at 11:30 we still needed a microscope! This is called 'exponential' growth. Many people have trouble understanding exponential growth because we're used to things growing 'linearly' - the same amount from one day to the next, like hair or grass or fingernails.

We expect the bottle to fill with bacteria as if we were filling it with water from a faucet. However, any time living things are allowed to reproduce freely, their numbers increase exponentially, not linearly. Moreover, when people - especially politicians and economists - talk about 'steady growth,' they mean exponential growth then, too.

If you were one of the bacteria, when do you suppose you'd start to worry about overcrowding? Would that leave you enough time to do anything about it?

Now imagine that just before 12:00, we bring in three more bottles. If we can help the bacteria to spill over into the other containers, they'll have four times as much space as they've ever had before!

How much time after 12:00 do you think this will give them? By 12:01 the bacteria in the first bottle have doubled to fill the second bottle.

At 12:02, all four bottles are full!

Many aspects of our environmental situation are similar to the bacteria's position in this story. For example, the human population of the world has doubled twice in the past hundred years. Energy consumption is doubling about four times faster than that, and the number of automobiles in the world is increasing ten times faster than population.

These are just a few examples. Any time you hear that something is increasing by a percentage - say, 5% per year - that means it's growing exponentially. There's an easy way to figure out how quickly something will double when it's growing exponentially. Just divide 70 by the percent increase, and you've got the doubling time. For example, if you hear that the population of your town is growing by 2% per year, that means it will double in just 35 years!

It works in reverse, too: divide 70 by the doubling time to find the growth rate. If you hear that U.S. population is due to double in 70 years, you know that it's increasing at 1% per year.

Isn't it amazing that just a 1% annual increase can cause a doubling in 70 years?

Remember this 'Rule of 70' whenever you hear that something is growing by some percentage, or that something is growing steadily. That means it's going to double - and probably sooner than you think!

When our consumption of a resource (energy, for instance) grows steadily, the doubling time takes on an even scarier meaning: during that time we use up more of the resource than in all of history before that time!

In the physical realm of nature, such growth usually shows up where illness or death can be found. The atomic bomb, or cancer, for example, follows such an exponential growth pattern. Exponential growth usually ends with the death of the organism from which it depends. The interest rate, which is the money we all have to pay to borrow money, is another example of this logarithmic growth.

Today's growth imperative, as measured by the GDP is based solely and alone on the capital constraint of interest rate growth.

If the earth is unable to sustain approximately 7,3 billion people at an acceptable standard of living, how can we hope to support 9 billion or 12 billion? How can we expect to improve their standard of living when there's less of everything to go around?

Faster Product Cycles

The industry is using the perpetual technique to create either products, which last only 1-2 years, or they are frequently modifying or upgrading the product. Releasing new product updates every year makes the consumer feel they have an outdated product and with a bit of smart advertising, they lure them into buying the new stuff.

How often have you changed your cell phone in the last ten years? What functions are you using? How about the latest washer and dryer, cooking stove, coffee machine or home stereo? Have you already the newest toilet seat, that softly glides down without a smash? When the industry releases a brand new product, they make sure not to include all the features and options that would make this product outstanding and lasting. Some features are released over time as you can see with the endless software updates these days.

Yes, innovations happen, and sometimes you have to break with the past and release something entirely new that's not compatible with your old device. However, that's not happening every year. A great example is the CD ROM drives that came on the market a long time ago. First, you had the single speed, next year the double speed, the following year the quad speed. After that, each year the rate increased, up to 16 and 32. The speed did not matter any longer, and other features were added for example faster-writing speed and so on.

Ask your grandfather or grandma when they bought shoes 30-40 years ago. They were made from beautiful leather, and lasted ten years at least. They were not cheap, and they had to be fixed from the shoe maker with new soles once a while. However, calculate the costs of shows today. There are almost as much as expensive, but they last maybe just a year or two. Sneakers are the worst of all. They are entirely made in China these days for a few dollars and sold for $100 and more. The material is mostly synthetic and glued together. The show industry releases a new sneaker almost every months - check your local Footlocker store.

The next big flaw in this system is the repair issue. Most electronic components can no longer be repaired at all. If only one little thing fails, you have to toss it into the garbage. If you do want it to be repaired, you end up with at least 50% of the purchase price. In many cases, the repair price exceeds what it is worth now.

Robbing Method #14 - Competition

"What kind of competition is there in your body? Suppose your brain said 'I'm the most important organ, and the liver said 'I am, and I want to go in a free enterprise-system.' You would rot away in a month, if every organ of your body, were out for itself." - Jacque Fresco, American futurist and social engineer

There is nothing to say against a good soccer match or any other sport, where kids are engaged in a playful form of competition. However, the teaching mentality in school to beat each other, with the effect of increasing isolation, is cruel and devastating to their life.

When they have to compete to start their career, the beautiful life they could have later on - together and in harmony with others - is already set up to fail. Kids from day one compete in a playful manner, but they also have an inherent sense of helping their fellow friends. This is merely a part of being human. It's a build in recognition from nature and spirit that every person, even those look different, are connected. It ensures that we as people love each other and therefore help each other.

Competition is to self-esteem as sugar is to teeth. Most people lose in most competitive encounters, and it's obvious why that causes self-doubt. However, even winning doesn't build character; it just lets a child gloat temporarily. Studies have shown that feelings of self-worth become dependent on external sources of evaluation as a result of competition: Your value is defined by what you've done. [21]

You're a good person in proportion to the number of people you've beaten.

In a competitive culture, a child is told that it isn't enough to be good - he must triumph over others. Success comes to be defined as victory, even though these two are very different things. Even when the child manages to win, the whole affair, psychologically speaking, becomes a vicious circle. The more they compete, the more they need to compete to feel good about themselves.

Competition often makes kids anxious, and that interferes with concentration. Second, competition doesn't permit them to share their talents and resources as cooperation does, so they can't learn from one another. Finally, trying to be ‚Number One' distracts them from what they're supposed to be learning.

Competition is a recipe for hostility. By definition, not everyone can win a contest. If one child wins, another cannot. It means that each child comes to regard others as obstacles to his or her success.

The concept of competition is so normalized these days that most people would instantly argue, that this is a good thing - even necessary. However, as a second thought, they also see the business world too. For example, it is widely discussed how much salary for a CEO is appropriate. There will always be pro and cons. No sum is ever to satisfy all parties. People get lost in numbers and other irrelevant facts, but don't understand that the fundamental concept of competition is the problem, to begin with.

Competition turns into war when we reach the business arena. How much attention goes away from making a great product or service into beating another firm? How much money is lost in productivity when companies work against each other? In the long run, if you have a competitor, you have to put them out of business or buy them. If you don't, you run into the problem of cutting prices to stay competitive. Of course, the other companies do these strategies as well, and so it's a losing position for all parties.

To stay afloat, companies are practicing so-called anti-competitive strategies. For example, dumping, where a company sells a product in a competitive market at a loss.

Though the company loses money for each sale, it hopes to force other competitors out of the market, after which the company would be free to raise prices for a higher profit.

Another method is exclusive dealing, where a retailer or wholesaler is obliged by contract to only purchase from the contracted supplier. Then there is price fixing, where companies collude to set prices, effectively dismantling the free market. Alternatively, the refusal to deal, e.g., two companies agree not to use a particular vendor.

Then companies look to divide territories, an agreement by two companies to stay out of each other's way and reduce competition in the agreed-upon areas. Alternatively, they limit pricing, where a monopolist sets the price at a level intended to discourage entry into a market.

Furthermore, there is the strategy of resale price maintenance, where resellers are not allowed to set prices independently.

How can a company - running with a competitive core concept - ever turn their success into wealth for itself and the people that work for the company? The only way out is to create a market monopoly, which is so cleverly constructed that the government won't break it up. However, when you have a monopoly in the market, something interesting is happening. Most companies are no longer investing in making their product or service better. They lean back, reap the money, and divide it by the owners - in most cases shareholders. The workers go out empty-handed, again.

The great industrial revolution was promising the reduction of heavy work and a better living standard. With the concept of competition, forced by the monetary system, this advantage is impossible.

Robbing Method #15 - Monopolies & Cartels

„Manufacturing and commercial monopolies owe their origin not to a tendency imminent in a capitalist economy but to governmental interventionist policy directed against free trade and laissez faire."
- Ludwig von Mises, Austrian School economist

A fast-growing number of Americans know that their country has a monopoly problem, and that wealth, power, and control are increasingly concentrated in the hands of the few.

A monopoly exists when a specific person or enterprise is the only supplier of a particular commodity. Monopolies are characterized by a lack of viable substitute goods and the possibility of a high monopoly price well above the seller's marginal cost that leads to a high monopoly profit. The verb 'monopolize' refers to the process by which a company gains the ability to raise prices or exclude competitors. In economics, a monopoly is a single seller. In law, a monopoly is a business entity that has significant market power, that is, the ability to charge overly high prices.22

A cartel is a group of formally independent producers whose goal is to increase their collective profits using price fixing, limiting supply, or other restrictive practices. Cartels typically control selling prices, but some are organized to control the costs of purchased inputs.

The 1913 Federal Reserve Act legalized the private credit-monopoly of an international cartel.

Congress does not audit the Federal Reserve because the private bank is not a government agency. The international cartel has the appearance of a governmental organization because the Federal Reserve has a legal partnership with the government; U.S. law backs the cartel. Over the years, additional regulations have re-enforced the collaboration and removed the original restrictions.

It is common for cartels to form partnerships with governments: the Organization of Petroleum Exporting Countries [OPEC] is an oil cartel that allied with the U.S. government in 1961. The oil cartel agreed to peg the price of oil to the dollar.

Governments go into partnership with banking cartels so that politicians can spend without set limits. After the dollar's tie to gold was cut in 1971, the greatest creditor-nation went on a spending spree and has never looked back. The United States is now the greatest debtor-nation in world history.

On 23 December 1924, a group of leading international businessmen gathered in Geneva for a meeting that would alter the world for decades to come. Present were top representatives from all the major light bulb manufacturers, including Germany's Osram, the Netherlands' Philips, France's Compagnie des Lampes, and the United States' General Electric. As revelers hung Christmas lights elsewhere in the city, the group founded the Phoebus cartel, a supervisory body that would carve up the worldwide incandescent light bulb market, with each national and regional zone assigned its manufacturers and production quotas. It was the first cartel in history to enjoy a truly global reach.

The Phoebus cartel enjoyed a genuinely global reach. The U.S. company General electric was itself not a member but was represented through its overseas subsidiaries. To protect their cartel, they threatened other companies that had longer lasting bulbs on the market. They would bad mouth them, blocking the retail chain or as a last resort buy them.

The cartel's grip on the lightbulb market lasted only into the 1930s. Its far more enduring legacy was to engineer a shorter lifespan for the incandescent light bulb. By early 1925, this became codified at 1,000 hours for a pear-shaped household bulb, a marked reduction from the 1,500 to 2,000 hours that had previously been common.

It wasn't just a matter of making an inferior or sloppy product; anybody could have done that. However, to create one that reliably failed after an agreed-upon 1,000 hours took some doing over many years. The household lightbulb in 1924 was already technologically sophisticated: The light yield was considerable; the burning time was easily 2,500 hours or more. By striving for something less, the cartel would systematically reverse decades of progress! In the end, you pay a higher price for a lousy product.[23]

Word has finally gotten out that corn syrup turns up in almost every candy and soda, and is as addictive as crack. What about Hand sanitizers? Ethanol car fuel? That's all corn, too. Making rubber tires? You'll need cornstarch. Spark plugs? Corn. Drywall? Corn. You can't build a car or a house without corn.

The king of American corn is Monsanto, a biotech company. They built their empire on a pretty dull one-two punch: weed killer and seeds.[24]

The weed killer, Roundup, is the biggest selling herbicide in the world. The seeds are genetically engineered corn seeds that are immune to Roundup. If you want to grow corn and kill weeds that hurt the corn, Monsanto has the best product on the market by a mile. That's why 80 percent of all corn planted in the U.S. goes into the ground with Monsanto's trademark on it.

However, plants will be plants and make more seeds, so the farmers don't have to keep buying Monsanto seeds year after year, right? Don't be silly. Monsanto's not going to let their money run away like that. Their first plan was to incorporate something called a "Terminator" gene that automatically sterilizes the plant so it can't make any more seeds. Then farmers have to buy new seeds every time they plant.

People objected to this quite a bit for some reason, forcing Monsanto to back down and instead make farmers sign a contract saying that they won't use the seeds the plants produce or they get sued. So instead of screwing farmers with a terminator gene, they're just asking the farmers to agree to screw themselves.

Guess what happens to your crops if you don't buy Monsanto's seeds, and your field is nearby a field with Monsanto seeds? Of course, the wind eventually will blow some of the seeds over and contaminate it. When Monsanto finds out that these fields have their seeds without having bought it from them, they either sue the farmer or tell him to buy their seeds to avoid legal consequences. In the end, you eat a product and no longer food, which is more expensive and a health threat.

A few more examples with numbers:

- Amazon sells 74 percent of all e-books sold online, and it sells 64 percent of all print books sold online. [25]
- Google controls 64 percent of all desktop searches and 94 percent of all global and mobile tablet searches.
- Intel controls some 98 percent of the microprocessor market in servers and about 93 percent in notebooks.
- China's vitamin cartel controls 100 percent of the market for U.S. Vitamin C, which is also known as ascorbic acid and which is used in almost all preserved foods.
- Recent mergers have left four carriers - American, United, Delta, and Southwest - with control over 80 percent of the market.
- Home Depot and Lowes control 90 percent of the home improvement store business.
- Walmart, controls 72 percent of warehouse clubs and super centers in the entire United States.
- Two firms, Dean Foods and the Dairy Farmers of America control as much as 80-90 percent of the milk supply chain in some states and wield substantial influence across the entire industry. [26]

Robbing Method #16 - Corporate Welfare

„The greatest weapon of mass destruction is corporate economic globalization." - Kenny Ausubel, Social entrepreneur, author, and filmmaker

Corporate welfare is a general term that refers to financial assistance, tax advantages, or other support given to corporations and other business entities by the United States government.[27]

Unlike welfare payments are given to individuals, the corporate welfare system is not intended to prevent poverty or raise the standard of living. Instead, the federal government awards payments to specific industries or companies in the form of subsidies, grants, contracts, and other aid. Due to the wide range of interests, the system is not monitored or controlled by a single Congressional committee.[28]

Only about 12 percent of federal spending goes to individuals and families - an increasing portion goes to corporate handouts.

When corporations get special handouts from the government – subsidies and tax breaks – it costs you. It means you have to pay more in taxes to make up for these hidden expenses. Also, the government has less money for schools and roads, Medicare and other social expenses.

When you pay taxes, you expect that money to go toward ensuring the greater good of society. Taxes pay for things like roads, schools, and hospitals, all of which are mutually beneficial to people from all walks of society.

One thing you probably don't expect your tax money to fund is bailouts for corporations that turn around and incorporate in another country to avoid paying taxes. Unfortunately, that happens more frequently than you might imagine, and it's all thanks to corporate welfare.[29]

Big Business Wins Big

Between 2000 and 2015, two-thirds of corporate welfare subsidies went to fewer than 600 large companies.

Even federal contractors receive loans, loan guarantees, and bailout assistance. Boeing, General Electric, and Bechtel have all collected billions of dollars from the federal government since 2000. Large banks and banks outside of the United States are also primary beneficiaries of corporate welfare.[30]

Small Businesses Can't Compete

Even though small businesses are considered by many to be the backbone of our economy, accounting for 54% of all sales in the United States, as well as the lion's share of job growth since the early 1990s, funding from the Small Business Administration is a fraction of that of corporate welfare.

It does not provide direct loans to small businesses; instead, it gives guidelines for small business loans from lending institutions. You know, those big banks getting all the bailouts.

It provides a significant challenge to small businesses trying to get off the ground, as they can't compete with huge corporations where decisions are made, knowing the government considers them too big to fail.

It's not just banks and government contractors who receive the benefit of tax money to fund their institutions. Private colleges accept private donations that allow their donor's significant tax breaks. Agricultural subsidies originally meant to help farmers avoid going out of business during poor growing seasons, instead encourage overproduction of commodities that may not even be needed.

In fact, 50 of the Forbes 400 wealthiest people in America had received farm subsidies before the 2014 Farm Bill went into effect. Private security is sold to private individuals, but backup comes in the form of a taxpayer-funded police response.

The finance sector is one of the biggest beneficiaries of corporate welfare. In 2008 alone, banks received $700 billion from the Troubled Asset Relief Fund (TARP).

What's more troubling is a University of Michigan study found that the more political ties a particular bank had to the federal government, the more likely it was to receive TARP funds, and also the more TARP funds it was possible to win.

According to the study, "research shows that TARP investment amounts were positively related to banks' political contributions and lobbying expenditures, and that, overall, the effect of political influence was most active for poorly performing banks."

The oil, gas, and coal industries get billions in their special tax breaks. Big Agribusiness receives farm subsidies. Big Pharma gets their subsidy in the form of a ban on government using its bargaining power under Medicare to negotiate lower drug prices. Also, hedge-fund and private-equity managers get a particular tax loophole that treats their income as capital gains, at a lower tax rate than ordinary income.

Corporate Welfare is Increasing

According to The Cato Institute, corporate welfare handouts shot all the way up to $92 billion as of 2002. Most of those subsidies were secured by companies in industries like energy - which are some of the most profitable entities in the history of the world. As one writer at Forbes points out, cutting these vast subsidies would be a great way to help balance the national budget, but it is never put into action, and much less even considered.[31]

More recently, subsidy tracking group Good Jobs First released a 2014 report detailing where exactly taxpayer dollars are being funneled, and which states are the most likely to divvy up handouts. There are some surprises in the report, but many details won't come as much of a shock at all. New York and Washington were the top two states for handing out corporate subsidies, with New York alone topping more than $20 billion across nearly 69,000 individual handouts. The data also shows that roughly 75% of disclosed subsidy dollars have gone to 965 big companies. The total known value of subsidies across the country came out at an estimated $110 billion, although it's likely more.

From its data, Good Jobs First was able to identify the top 100 recipients of corporate subsidies, dominated by transportation and natural resource companies. Here are the top eight companies from that list, and the total known amount in subsidies they are receiving.[32]

Why are these Companies Receive Your Tax Money?

Nike — $2.03 Billion

Nike, based in the Portland suburb of Beaverton, Oregon, has taken in more than $2 billion in government appropriations, spanning 75 individual subsidies. Spanning the globe regarding the scope and reach, Nike isn't exactly strapped for cash, so making the case that the company is in need of government assistance can be difficult.

Royal Dutch Shell — $2.04 Billion

As a petroleum company, Shell has been reaping profits like the world has never seen before, along with industry cohorts like Exxon Mobil. Many consumers have had to find ways to adjust as gas prices continue to rise, along with production costs of plastics and other materials. All the while, major oil companies have been sitting back and watching profits pile up.

Fiat Chrysler Automobiles — $2.06 Billion

Fiat, now the owner of Chrysler, has been receiving a considerable chunk of taxpayer cash to help with its vehicle production worldwide. The government has ponied over more than $2 billion to the Italian-based automaker, which it has used to help prop up brands like Dodge, Ram, and Chrysler here in the states.

Ford — $2.52 Billion

It doesn't get much more "American" than the Ford Motor Company, which itself has allocated $2.52 billion in government funding as of late. Spread across 193 separate appropriations, the subsidies have been able to help Ford recover from the financial crisis and adapt to a world that looks more and more like it will have fewer cars on the road in coming years.

General Motors — $3.58 Billion

Detroit's own General Motors was found to be getting $3.58 billion in subsidies, coming in from 320 individual appropriations. Having survived bankruptcy on the backs of the taxpayers in 2009, GM took drastic measures to return itself to profitability. Several brands were cut from under the GM umbrella, leaving just four still in production.

Intel — $3.87 Billion

The pride of Santa Clara, California, Intel is a maker of semiconductor microchips used in computers all across the world. The company was one of the big drivers behind the computing revolution of the 1980s and 1990s, and its founding dates all the way back to 1968. Intel is also on the receiving end of large amounts of government cash, with totals reaching $3.87 billion from 59 individual subsidies.

Alcoa — $5.64 Billion

You may not know Alcoa by name, but there's probably at least one product with Alcoa aluminum in it somewhere in your home. As the world's third largest producer of aluminum, Alcoa has an extensive history dating back to 1886 when it was first founded in Pittsburgh, Pennsylvania. The company has received $5.64 billion across 99 subsidies according to Find Good Jobs' report, which has helped the company go on to secure lucrative contracts for projects, like building jet engine parts.

Boeing — $13.18 Billion

The top welfare recipient of them all is aerospace giant Boeing, which has operations spread all across the country building aircraft and working on numerous Department of Defense projects. The amount of work Boeing does for the federal government no doubt plays a part in the number of subsidies the company has been able to secure, but Boeing has also played hardball with local jurisdictions to get enormous tax breaks. With more than $13 billion coming in from 148 handouts, Boeing has thoroughly entrenched itself in the interest of the government and taxpayers.

Despite the immense amount of money the company receives, it has still gone on to hold cities hostage in tax negotiations, threatening to remove jobs and open up shop in friendlier climates. The real issue isn't the government's size. It's whom government is for. Much of government is no longer working for the vast majority it's intended to serve. If the government was responding to the public's interest instead of the moneyed interests, it would be providing more support for communities, families, and individuals who need it the most.

There's no reason any corporations should be on the dole, or that your hard-earned dollars should be going to them for no reason but their political clout.

Robbing Method #17 - Employment

"Many people quit looking for work when they find a job."
- Zig Ziglar, American author and motivational speaker

When it comes to employment, most people consider it the only way to make a living. Sadly, in most cases, it's the worst you can do with your life. Steve Pavlina, a personal life coach, expressed various interesting points, which I have summarized below.

It's funny that when people reach a certain age, such as after graduating college, they assume it's time to go out and get a job. However, like many things the masses do, just because everyone does, it doesn't mean it's a good idea.

In fact, if you're reasonably intelligent, getting a job is one of the worst things you can do to support yourself. There are far better ways to make a living than selling yourself into indentured servitude.

Trading Your Time for Money

You only get paid when you're working. Have you ever considered that it might be better to be paid even when you're not working? Who taught you that you could only earn income while working? The key is to de-couple your value from your time.

You might think it's important to get a job to gain experience. However, that's like saying you should play golf to get experience playing golf. You gain experience from living, regardless of whether you have a job or not. A job only gives you experience at that job, but you gain "experience" doing just about anything, so that's no real benefit at all.

The problem with getting experience from a job is that you usually repeat the same limited experience over and over. You learn a lot in the beginning and then stagnate. It forces you to miss other experiences that would be much more valuable. Also, if your limited skill set ever becomes obsolete, then your experience won't be worth squat. In fact, ask yourself what the experience you're gaining right now will be worth in 20-30 years. Will your job even exist then or will it be already automated in the coming years?

At the turn of the century, about 38 percent of the labor force worked on farms. By the end of the century, that figure was less than 3 percent. Likewise, the percentage who worked in goods-producing industries, such as mining, manufacturing, and construction, decreased from 31 to 19 percent of the workforce. The next revolution is already happening in the service industry.

Slavery never ended, they just gave it a new name - employee!

Have you noticed how your local bank has changed their way of dealing with customers? Artificial intelligence is almost real for prime time and will soon replace entire industrial sectors. For example, you can now take a photo with your smartphone from your skin, upload it on the Internet and get a skin analysis back in seconds!

Google recently released the so-called 'Google Duplex' system, which is capable of calling a business and making an appointment for its client. Duplex is the culmination of all Google's AI and machine learning skills. It uses the Assistant platform to process and respond to human beings. Google Duplex, will probably soon replace all major call center operations.

Employees Pay the Highest Taxes

Employee income is the most heavily taxed there is. In the USA you can expect that about half your salary will go to taxes. The tax system is designed to disguise how much you're giving up because your employer pays some of those taxes, and some are deducted from your paycheck. However, you can bet that from your employer's perspective, all of those taxes are considered part of your pay, as well as any other compensation you receive such as benefits. Even the rent for the office space you consume is considered, so you must generate that much more value to cover it. You might feel supported by your corporate environment, but keep in mind that you're the one paying for it.

It isn't hard to understand why employees pay the most in taxes relative to their income. After all, who has more control over the tax system? Business owners and investors or employees?

You only get paid a fraction of the real value you generate. Your actual salary may be more than triple what you're paid, but most of that money you'll never see. It goes straight into other people's pockets. On top of it all, you have to beg for an increase in your salary - it's entirely outside of your control.

Was It Ever Secure?

Many employees believe getting a job is the safest and most secure way to support themselves. If that has any truth to it, it may have been a long time ago.

Does putting yourself in a position where someone else can turn off all your income just by saying two words ("You're fired") sound like a safe and secure situation for you? You can't have security if you don't have control, and employees have the least power over anyone.

The Loss of Freedom

It takes much effort to tame a human being into an employee. The first thing you have to do is break the human's independent will. An excellent way to do this is to give them a weighty policy manual filled with nonsensical rules and regulations. It leads the new employee to become more obedient, fearing to be disciplined at any minute for something incomprehensible. As part of their obedience training, employees must be taught how to dress, talk, move, and so on.[33]

127

Have you noticed that employed people have almost endless capacity to whine about problems at their companies? However, they don't want solutions - they want to vent and make excuses why it's all someone else's fault.

It's as if getting a job somehow drains all the free will out of people and turns them into spineless cowards. If you can't call your boss a jerk now and then without fear of getting fired, you're no longer free.

Many people with jobs have to deal with values conflicts with their employer. For instance, you might care about helping customers solve their problems, but maybe your employer wants you to push for more sales. Alternatively, you might value good health habits while your company succumbs to a culture of junk food and soda. Also, quite often employers have chaotically shifting values that are unclear, so you never know whether you're aligned with them or not.

A job can also tie you to a single location, but without a job, you can go wherever you want, whenever you want. You can even live on the road if you like. Even that loss of freedom does not sound it's related to money. If you take a closer look - it does. One way or another almost all things are related to money.

Robbing Method #18 - The Retirement Gamble

"Among other reasons, 401(k)s and IRAs involve putting money into an investment vehicle over which investors have little control. And since most people end up choosing mutual funds as their primary investment within these plans, playing the lottery would be a better way to go." - Robert Kiyosaki, American businessman and author

There are several ways how the government subtly helps Wall Street fund its addiction to speculation and stock market gambling. One of the ways it does that is through the 401k tax provision.

It shouldn't surprise you that the 401K, marketed to us as a retirement plan, is just a cash cow for Wall Street. After all, the 401k started as a tax loophole for executive pay.

A 401k retirement "account" allows you to make money on financial income without being taxed on it until later. For instance, if, one year, you put 100$ in your 401k, the income tax you would've paid on it is suspended. Not until after you've retired and pulled out that money will you pay income taxes on it - long after you've made interest, dividends, and other money with your untaxed money.

On top of that, your employer will get certain tax deductions and credits for setting up and directly contributing to an employee 401k plan. When an employer sets up a 401k, a wall street firm will charge them a specific fee. However, the government gives the employer a tax credit to cover some or part of the cost. It's mostly the federal govern-ment subsidizing 401k Management firms.[34]

The worse part is the tax-free income of the 401k. All the money made in a 401k can get reinvested and doesn't get taxed until you want to spend it. That might make sense for business taxes that pay only on profits, but not for personal taxes. Personal income taxes, you pay on all income.

A 401k locks you into handing your money to Wall Street firms by specifying what you can't do with a 401k. You can't use your 401k savings to invest in your friend's small business. You can take out a loan against your 401k, but still have to pay it back to wall street - with interest!. Unless that small business is listed on the New York stock exchange. Once Wall Street has your money via your 401k, they have it until you retire, unless you're willing to pay a considerable fee, of course.

Because the government incentives employers to have as many employees to participate as possible, they offer matching funds (which are tax-deductible) that employees wouldn't get if they don't participate in the 401k. If an individual employee doesn't cooperate, he is losing money because of the government subsidies.

So what does this all amount to? The federal government pays employers to set up 401k "retirement" funds that can only invest in financial assets that Wall Street firms control, pays employers to get as many people to participate as possible, and then gives employees tax breaks to go along with it.

You might think I'm exaggerating the importance of the 401k in directing money to Wall Street. So let's look at the numbers. The 401k law went into effect in 1980. In that year, the percentage of people who owned stock was 13%. A slight dip from 15% in 1970. By 1989, the number was 32% - more than double as nine years earlier. By 1998 over half of the country owned stock [35]. There is significant financial wealth to be held with 401k's, worth nearly 3 trillion dollars. That is much money to be sloshing around in Wall Street's computer banks. As you can imagine that 3 trillion dollars mean many fees for managing all that wealth.[36]

There is no problem with people entering the wall street casino willingly. However, now we incentivize people to join it. Requiring people to participate it to make sure they get all the tax breaks they wouldn't receive otherwise. This requirement means that people who are not qualified to manage their investments are forced into it.

The irony here is dripping. First, we are assumed to be too stupid to save for our retirement correctly, so we have to have tax breaks that incentivize us to give money to Wall Street to save for retirement. However, once we decide to hand our money over, then suddenly we are magically smart enough to manage our stock portfolio. As you can imagine, most aren't educated, nor have enough time to make informed decisions. This disparity reflects poorly on those who most need a retirement plan. Only the highest educated and most familiar regularly beat the system and maximize their gains.

In a Nutshell

Your investment options are limited. The plan options that you have depend on the ability of your company's investment options. It limits you from choosing investment plans that will best suit your investing style. If you are working for a small company, you might find an individual retirement account (IRA) more beneficial for your retirement plans, wherein you can choose your investments, instead of being limited with your options.

Your withdrawals are restricted. Once you have started your contribution to your 401(k) plan, you can only withdraw under special circumstances, and before you are 59 years and six months old. There are certain conditions that you have to remember before withdrawal. Your employment must have already been terminated from the company, you must have experienced permanent disability, or you have been undergoing financial hardship. Even financial hardships should also be defined, such that if you are unable to pay for your rents. Once you qualify for an early withdrawal, you should still pay for taxes, and you will be penalized by 10 percent of the total amount for early withdrawal.

Robbing Method #19 - The Scientific Method

"The saddest aspect of life right now is that science gathers knowledge faster than society gathers wisdom." - Isaac Asimov, American science fiction writer

As by definition from the dictionary, the scientific method is a method of research in which a problem is identified, relevant data are gathered, a hypothesis is formulated from these data, and the hypothesis is empirically tested.

So it all starts with a hypothesis, and very often the starting point is by observing the environment. However, since quantum science was added to our knowledge, the observer is not independent of the observed and influences the outcome. The scientific method, therefore, is nothing else than a concept and not the truth, as most people believe.

Besides that, the scientific method is only the latest concept in a long cycle of evolution of civilizations. Civilizations have always come and go. Viewed over more extended periods of time they always seem to cycle like a sinus curve between a material and a spiritual concept. Bruce Lipton describes the core concept of these civilizations as follows:

A culture's character is determined by its answers three perennial questions:

- Why are we here?
- How did we get here?
- How do we make the best of being here?

Throughout history, different civilizations have had different answers to these questions. Whenever the answers changed, culture also altered to accommodate the new answers.

We call the belief system in these answers the basal paradigm of a civilization, its fundamental ideas. Whoever provides the answers for a civilization also becomes the provider of all other truths for that civilization. So, as the answers change, the truths change, and people's belief in who bears the truth changes, changing the character of cultures over time.[37]

Charles Darwin - The Theory of Evolution

Charles Darwin presented his theory of evolution, and a new civilization began. Science now had a valid understanding of how we got here. They saw that indeed the parents' traits were passed on to their offspring and that now and then you get a "weirdo" and that weirdo can create something different.

When Darwin said that we got here through accidents of evolution – a change of genetics creating weird organisms that followed on their path and together led to all the species – that made more sense to people than the story of Genesis. Within ten years of 1859, civilization changed, and scientific materialism emerged.

It had new answers for the perennial questions:

- How did we get here? Through random mutations.
- Why are we here? We are accidental tourists on the planet.
- How do we make the best of it? We are living in a struggle for existence that is based on the survival of the fittest.

It's a fundamental issue because it says we must go out there and work like crazy because if we don't, somebody else will beat us and kill us in the process.

The problem with scientific materialism is that it offers an end but no means. It's the law of the jungle. The means to survival are any way you can get there. You can use your brain and be Einstein or you can use an Uzi and be a brute. Either means can make you a leader.[38]

It's a civilization based on competition, not morality.

It's the environment we live in right now. Newtonian physics also failed to address the invisible realm that religion talks about; one doesn't need the spiritual realm to understand the material realm. As a result, people in this culture accumulate as much material as they possibly can to beat everybody else in the race for survival. Die with the most toys, and you win the game. The consequences? We have decimated the planet.

The Foundation of Science and Mathematics

Something else to consider here is that all the different sciences are connected to each other in building blocks that cement their belief systems. The foundation of all science is mathematics.

On top of that is physics; you can't have physics without mathematics. Physics leads to an understanding of chemistry, and chemistry to an understanding of biology. When you understand biology, you can get into psychology. These are the building blocks of our belief system, and it is predicated on Newtonian physics, which says that matter is primal.

This whole belief system is changing, however. It began to change when it went a little deeper. In 1953, the concept of a "potential" gene became real when scientists identified DNA. A chemical – well, what do you expect in a chemical, material world? We bought into the gene story and determined there's one last thing we must do: the Human Genome Project.

Human Genome Project

Between 1953 and 2001, while the Human Genome Project was underway, people started pulling away from the conventional medical profession. It wasn't fully working for them, and they began to explore alternative methods. We've learned that 50 percent or more of the population seek an alternative, complementary, or integrative medicine doctor over a conventional doctor.

People have lost belief in the system. Then the Human Genome Project pulled the rug out. It was supposed to verify the model that genes create life and to show us the more than 150,000 genes involved, but the project finished with only 23,000 genes. Something was amiss.

Seeking New Answers

So the reality is that at this very time there is upheaval. People are looking for new answers, and what we are discovering reveals something different about life.

For example, biology predicated on Newtonian physics, which is mechanical and physical, looks to something physical – that is, chemicals and drugs – to understand disease and healing. However, a new scientific reality, quantum physics, says that everything is made out of energy.

It is primal to matter and shapes matter. Another myth of material science is that genes control biology, making us victims of our heredity. The new science of epigenetics, however, says that genes do not control our life; our perceptions, emotions, beliefs, and attitudes rewrite our genetic code.

Through our perceptions, we can modify every gene in our body and create thirty thousand variations from every gene just by the way we respond to life. In short, we are leaving behind a reality of victimization (by our genes) and moving into the fact that our mind – our consciousness, the immaterial realm – influences our experience and potential.

The new theory of evolution is based on cooperation and community, not Darwinian individualism. Our erroneous theories and belief systems have us killing one another and robbing the earth when it turns out that according to the new science, such competitive, survivalist behavior is precipitating catastrophe. We haven't understood the nature of the community.

The beliefs we have been living with are outdated!

Robbing Method #20 - Advertisement

„Advertising may be described as the science of arresting the human intelligence long enough to get money from it." - Stephen Butler Leacock, Canadian teacher and political scientist

If you consider the previously introduced robbing methods as monstrous, the next level of mind control is nothing else than frightful. The result is either to steal money from your pocket or even worse, eliminate the ability to control the money that flows into your pocket. All that is done by manipulating your mind into believing things which you are not aware.

When asked about these subliminal effects of advertising most people argue, that's the way it is, or it's normal. It's mostly perceived as facts, which are only beliefs and concepts that are transparent to you.

It's like having your beliefs written in stone - there are here to stay for your entire life without the slightest moment of recognition that you put it there in the first place. You did not create them, but you took it over and unconsciously decided to make it your truth.

Advertising doesn't cause addictions. However, it does create a climate of denial, and it contributes mightily to a belief in the quick fix, instant gratification, the dreamworld, and escape from all pain and boredom. All of this is part of what addicts believe and what we hope for when we reach for our particular substance. Addiction begins with the hope that something "out there" can instantly fill up the emptiness inside. Advertising is all about this false hope.[39]

Advertisement - A Money Fix For Corporations

Within the area of the first industrial revolution, products could be produced at a much lower cost. They were suddenly available to a much bigger market - the middle class - people that worked in the factories and fabrics. These were the times where the United States had the most significant expansion. Productivity was going through the roof.

However, there was something that started to bother people that were running these giant fabrics and factories. When they were thinking about the future, they realized that there would be a time, not so far in the future, where almost all people have everything that was produced. It was a scary moment, and there was a need for a solution; otherwise the fate of most companies was doomed. The same time the industrial revolution happened, another revolution occurred in the area of the mind - Freud's psychoanalysis.

Sigmund Freud, the founder of psychoanalysis, changed the perception of the human mind and its workings profoundly.

His influence on the 20th century is widely regarded as massive. Freud's theories on the perception of the human mind, and the ways public relations agencies and politicians have used this during the last 100 years for their engineering of consent. Among the main characters are Freud himself and his nephew Edward Bernays, who was the first to use psychological techniques in advertising. He is often seen as the father of the public relations industry.[40]

Architects of the Consumer Mind

Edward Bernays who invented Public Relations in the 1920s, being the first person to take Freud's ideas to manipulate the masses. Those in power in post-war America used Freud's ideas about the unconscious mind to try and control the masses.

Bernays was among the first to understand that one of the implications of the subconscious mind was, that it could be appealed to sell products and ideas. You no longer had to offer people what they needed; by linking your brand with their more profound hopes and fears, you could persuade them to buy what they dreamed.

In Bernays's future, you didn't buy a new car because the old one stopped running; you bought a more modern one to increase your Self-esteem, or a lower slung one to enhance your sense of your sex-appeal. You didn't choose a pair of running shoes for comfort or practicality; you did so because somewhere deep inside you, you felt they might liberate you to 'Just Do It.'

You didn't vote for a political party out of duty, or because you believed it had the best policies to advance the common good; you did so because of a secret feeling that it offered you the most likely opportunity to promote and express yourself.

Bernays himself emerges as a remarkable character. He not only was able to sell the American people anything - he made it cool for women to smoke and for children to love soap and for eggs to accompany bacon - his skills also could win elections and change the course of foreign policy.

The principles of Freudianism, initially through Bernays, had a profound effect on corporations and governments, and led directly to the new all-pervasive ideas of market research and focus groups - psychoanalysis of products and ideas. Those forces have shaped the way we live and think and vote today.

Apart from the fact that the purchase of every canned drink or deodorant requires us to locate the hero inside yourself, our television, for example, is increasingly dedicated - from Trisha to Changing Rooms to Pop Idol - to Self-help and Self-improvement and Self-creation.

We find collective comfort in celebrity; we like to colonize another Self and treat it like our own. Our bestseller lists, from Harry Potter to Bridget Jones to A Boy Called It, reflect different kinds of wish-fulfillment.[41]

Meanwhile, with the power of the Internet and the massive advantage of intelligent computer networks, advertising for businesses became a scientific approach. The tracking of every move you make, every product you buy and every comment you make is analyzed and computed into an individual customer profile. Meanwhile, artificially intelligent software programs generate in fractions of second precise consumer models out of an enormous amount of information.

If you use Facebook, Twitter and other social networks then you give away this information in little pieces free in exchange for using these services. These networks are massive customer profiling operations that gather billions, soon trillions of single data pieces and spit them out on the other end as almost perfect customized and individualized profiles.

You may not understand the significance of a data package that tells the advertising company how a $150 sneaker is linked to other shopping behavior. For example t-shirts, cars, health and so on. From such a data package an advertiser could make accurate predictions about this person, that is so mind-boggling, that companies could give away such multi-billion services for free. Facebook and Twitter make their money entirely with advertising, which is based on your profile.

The original intent of service got so far lost, that every single decision and the analytical piece of data is entirely used to sell a product. To sell, even more, very advanced sophisticated mathematical models, and in-depth physiological, behavioral studies have to be invented. Meanwhile, only big corporations can afford it.

Coca Cola's internal marketing strategy was for a long time this: „to sell more Coke to more people more often".

This thinking model – based on control – not only leads to an emphasis on creating products that we don't need. Worse than that, it produces products that are designed to break down faster and more often. This approach does not work for a long time as customers will soon protest and switch to other companies. Meanwhile, the psychological induced individualization process has made us buy products, by believing that our current product is useless and outdated, and uncool the moment a newer model is released.

Marshall McLuhan once said that advertising is an environmental striptease for a world of abundance.

Robbing Method #21 - Instant Gratification

„We live in a day when the adversary stresses on every hand the philosophy of instant gratification. We seem to demand instant everything, including instant solutions to our problems. . .It was meant to be that life would be a challenge. To suffer some anxiety, some depression, some disappointment, even some failure is normal." - Boyd K. Packer, American religious leader and former educator

Instant gratification is the desire to experience pleasure or fulfillment without delay or deferment. It's when you want it - and you want it now. Our entire consumer culture has elevated immediate gratification to live's primary goal. No wonder the word wealth does not even exist in the vocabulary of most people.[42]

Instant gratification is based on our experience from centuries ago, where we were still living in the stage of gathers and hunters. At that age, food could not be preserved. Food was available only at the moment when we killed an animal. After it was eaten, there was another gap, as to when we would have another meal. So we ate only when food was available.

A research study conducted by Jonathan Cohen, a neuroscientist at Princeton University showed that instant gratification and delayed gratification activate different parts of the brain. Instant gratification enables the brains reward system – the region responsible for emotional decisions. Delayed gratification activates the pre-frontal cortex – the component responsible for rational decisions. The study shows that the emotional part of a brain overrides the rational part of the brain. [43]

The Stanford University conducted an interesting experiment known as the 'marsh-mellow experiment' in the late 1960 and early 1970 and led by psychologist Walter Mischel.

They gave 4-year-old kids a choice. They either get one marsh-mellow now or two marsh-mellows after waiting for a while. Most of the kids chose to get one marsh-mellow now instead of two later. The kids were then followed for years, how they did in school and how they fared in life. The kids who chose to wait for two marsh-mellows ended up doing much better in life compared to the impatient kids.[44]

In the past, we lived very close to nature, and we could not hunt in the night or in adverse weather conditions. Everything at that stage of life was very much in the moment and either spontaneous or based on necessity.

Forward a few hundred years into the 21. Century, our brains seem still operating from that area of time. We still purchase emotionally and strive for instant gratification. We always want to have every experience instantly.

This behavior prevents us from experiencing new inventions that we have made over the last few hundred years. We now can shop 24/7 and have almost unlimited food resources and variations to choose from. Having food available is no longer an issue, the problem now is distribution. The same is true for almost any other product we can now buy. If it's not available around the corner, we can order it via the Internet.

Billboards, slogans, banners, and shop signs assault the innocent pedestrian. The invisible fingers of the market manipulators are forever seeking to stimulate trivial desires and separate you from your hard-earned money, even enticing you to spend much more than you have through a credit system.

If people tend to consume too many soft drinks, eat too many fast meals, take too many medications, and buy too many things that they don't need for their well-being, it's because their sense of instant gratification is perpetually exploited. Neon signs, repetitive trigger words, colorful logos, and jingles influence ‚consumers'.

We buy emotional and justify it rationally. All form of advertising is using this fundamental behavior.

This exploitation of a need for instant gratification does more harm than merely empty bank accounts. All kinds of aberrant behavior arise from distraught people, including domestic abuse, suicide, and criminal activity to compensate for cash shortages.

The higher a person's need for instant gratification, the lower their emotional intelligence.

Another trick to manipulate your behavior into impulse purchase is the method of deliberately limiting the supply, or making only a few items of the product available for a specific time. It immediately triggers your survival instinct and shuts down your ability of rational thinking.

Scarcity is Artificially Created

Scarcity today is used as a political and economic weapon to keep you from seeing what is going on in the world. It continually narrows your perspective and attention. It keeps you in a state of contraction. There are enough resources, unlimited money and enough creative people on the planet to live in abundance right now. The interest payment of the US per year alone is enough to eliminate poverty immediately. Don't be fooled by the massive media and marketing machine saying otherwise.

Robbing Method #22 - Mind Control

"The conscious and intelligent manipulation of the organized habits and opinions of the masses is an important element in democratic society. Those who manipulate this unseen mechanism of society constitute an invisible government which is the true ruling power of our country.

We are governed, our minds are molded, our tastes formed, our ideas suggested, largely by men we have never heard of. This is a logical result of the way in which our democratic society is organized. Vast numbers of human beings must cooperate in this manner if they are to live together as a smoothly functioning society.

In almost every act of our daily lives, whether in the sphere of politics or business, in our social conduct or our ethical thinking, we are dominated by the relatively small number of persons...who understand the mental processes and social patterns of the masses. It is they who pull the wires which control the public mind."

- Edward L. Bernays, Austrian-American pioneer in the field of public relations and propaganda

Since the very moment you were born, society has imposed on you what to do, what to think and what to feel. If you don't follow the rules and laws of society, then you are bound to get into trouble.

Parents taught you to behave in specific ways. If you did, they would reward you, and if you didn't, they would punish you. Naturally, every child obeys its parents, because the child is dependent on the parents - it is a matter of survival, especially in its very early years.

In school, you were taught to think in specific ways. They taught you what to believe, but not how to develop your thinking. Everyone was taught the same. If we thought different than our classmates, teachers would tell us that we are bad students. They would give us bad grades and might even expel us from school. Therefore, as students, we learned to compromise our thinking and get away without causing trouble.[45]

Religion taught you to follow anything but your inner voice - scriptures, priests, gods. It taught you to have faith in others, but not to have confidence in yourself. Religion rewards you with the bliss of heaven if you follow the rules, or punished in hellfire if you don't. Who in their right mind would desire to be punished in hell? So, who wouldn't want to experience heaven?

Not surprisingly, we held religion in dear faith. The most common roots of the word religion take you back to the Latin word ,Re-Ligare.' ,Ligare' means ,to bind' or to ,connect.' Adding the ,re' before ,ligare' causes the word to mean ,Re-Bind' or ,Re-Connect.' [46] This is actually very revealing, and I devote an extra chapter in part III of this book.

Fear is the Best Weapon of all Manipulators

Parents, school, and religion used the same thing to make you do what they wanted you to do: fear. If you're going to manipulate anybody, first make them afraid. Once afraid, they will be ready to accept your offered suggestions.

This tactic is being continuously used in our everyday life, but we are unaware of it. Politicians are being elected by persuading the masses through the use of fear. Companies are selling their products by manipulating consumers' insecurities in advertising. Journalists influence public opinion by terrorizing people's minds. These are just a few examples.[47]

Fear is the best weapon of all great manipulators. It can move people to do anything, no matter how nonsensical it is.

People are programmed through centuries of hunting and gathering to be on alert for threats, and hard-wired to protect themselves from signs of danger. Sadly, humanity in general also seems to have developed a morbid fascination with the misfortune of others. In some way, seeing others suffer seems to make us feel better about our condition.

Those behind the media understand our more profound psychological needs and desires. They program what they think people want to watch, and as we affirm their judgment by continuing to digest stories demonizing alternative spirituality, the cycle of persecution continues.

Since the inception of propaganda, its practitioners have known that with enough repetition, it's possible to convince the public that almost anything is right – look at Goebells or Hitler.

A single piece of media often does not have a lasting effect on the human psyche, but the more you are bombarded by anti-cult sentiment, the more likely you are to believe that what you're being told is true.

Deliberate mind manipulation of the masses is, by itself, nothing new. Nearly a hundred years ago, our global mania for consumption was unleashed by the malevolent brilliance of Edward Bernays, known as the "father of public relations." Bernays was Sigmund Freud's nephew and used his uncle's insights into the subconscious to develop his new methods of mind control, designed to create the modern American consumer.

"We must shift America from a needs to a desires culture," declared Bernays' business partner, Paul Mazur. *"People must be trained to desire, to want new things, even before the old have been entirely consumed. We must shape a new mentality. Man's desires must overshadow his needs."*

In 1928, Bernays proudly described how his techniques for mental manipulation had permitted a small elite to control the minds of the American population:

The conscious and intelligent manipulation of the organized habits and opinions of the masses is an important element in democratic society. Those who manipulate this unseen mechanism of society constitute an invisible government that is the true ruling power of this country. We are governed, our minds molded, our tastes formed, our ideas suggested, largely by men we have never heard of. [48]

In almost every act of our daily lives, we are dominated by the relatively small number of persons, who pull the wires which control the public mind.

Bernays set in motion what we have all come to know as an essential part of our capitalist ecosystem: the use of mass media to promote roles, desires and status symbols that rake in profits for corporations.

The New Social Media Mind Control Tactics

B.J. Fogg has founded a field called "captology," derived from the acronym CAPT or "Computers As Persuasive Technology." At the ominously named Stanford Persuasive Tech Lab, he teaches freshly minted graduate students how to use technology to "change people's attitudes or behaviors."

His teachings have spawned the interfaces of our new daily routines: the chimes from our smartphones diverting our attention, the thumbs-up icon on our news feeds, and the ‚Like' statistics telling us how popular we are today. These are known as "hot triggers" which kick off behavioral loops in our subconscious. Successful apps, they teach, are those that trigger a momentary need, and then provide us with an instant solution. The solution sparks a microdose of endorphins in our brains. That feels good. So, like rats on a wheel, we find ourselves getting addicted, going back for more.[49]

Facebook has built its global empire of 2.23 billion active users[50] on this addictive routine. According to one of Fogg's students, Nir Eyal, Facebook's key trigger is FOMO: fear of missing out. Humans evolved in hunter-gatherer bands, where survival meant being part of the community. The social anxiety of missing what our friends are doing arises from deep within our hormonal system.

Facebook has been researching the extent of its power over our behavior, manipulating its users as guinea pigs. On election day in 2010, it sent "Go out and vote" reminders to more than 60 million users, causing an estimated 340,000 to vote who otherwise wouldn't have. If it chose to send these reminders to supporters of a particular party or candidate, it could easily flip an election without anyone knowing about it. Under current law, it wouldn't have to tell anyone what it was doing. In another experiment, which caused a public outcry, Facebook successfully manipulated the emotional state of 689,000 users by sending them either an excess of positive or negative terms in their news feeds.

The mind control doesn't stop at social media. Do you believe in your autonomy when you're carefully researching a topic and use Google to search for something? Think again. Psychologist Robert Epstein has unearthed the massive subliminal power of what he's called the Search Engine Manipulation Effect, or SEME.

This effect is based on the fact that when we search, we click half the time on one of the first two results, and more than 90% of our clicks are on the top ten links listed on the first page. There might be thousands of other web pages containing our keywords, but Google decides which ones we're going to read.

In many countries of the world, including the U.S., Google has a near monopoly over Internet searches. The search-ranking business is entirely unregulated, and courts have ruled that Google's right to rank search results however it please be protected as a form of free speech. If Google chose to swing the U.S. election, they could probably do so without anyone knowing about it.[51]

Your mind is continually manipulated without you recognizing it. Your decisions, habits, and desires are remotely engineered by programs that serve banks, governments, and large corporations. You lose complete control over your ethical values, and your life becomes that of a puppet. The worst part - you don't realize, and you even defending it, if questioned. Your money flies out faster of your pocket than you can think, mostly for goods and services you don't need.

The Current Monetary System - Summary

"Whoever controls the volume of money in any country is absolute master of all industry and commerce." - James A. Garfield, President of the United States

Now that you have made it here let us wrap up how the current monetary system operates, and how it affects you and the entire world.

Almost all countries today are using fiat money. Fiat money is money without intrinsic value established by the government by law. Another name for it is currency. You are not allowed to use any other form of money besides what has been declared by law from your government. Because it has no intrinsic value, it's simple to manipulate. Fiat money only works through the trust of the people who use it. No Fiat currency ever has survived! They all went to the value which they represent - zero! Never before in history has the entire world used fiat currency! It is the most significant monetary experiment and scam in history.

Most governments are not allowed by banks to establish their own money, which shows you where the real power lies. Therefore governments have to borrow it from the banks with interest. The interest can be tiny, but given the trillions of dollars, they lend it ends up as a vast amount. Governments are slaves to the banks and therefore all people that use these banks.

Central banks establish the interest rate, and therefore expand or shrink the market at their free will. In a society that is not regulated by central banks, the free market controls its prices automatically depending on the demand. Without central banks and interest, the cost of all goods and services are getting lower with each year and the purchasing power of each person increases. Without the manipulation of central banks, the level of abundance in a society increases all the time!

The interest that governments have to pay back to the banks does not exist. Therefore it needs to be created from the market. It means either higher taxes, higher prices or paying for services that used to be free. More and more areas of life have to be monetized to pay back the interest.

The interest payments lead to the goal of having a higher GDP - constant growth. This measurement is ingrained in our daily lives as one of the most profound facts. We all believe steady growth is the primary drive in life. But constant growth leads to less nature and therefore less room to live. It leads to more competition and hence more stress, depression and an ever increasing crime rate. The production of more useless staff and the increase of toxic trash that destroys nature and our food supply. It causes us to live in isolation to each other and an ever-increasing fear. It is the cause for new laws and regulations, that strip us piece by piece from our freedom. Constant growth is the death sentence of humanity and the earth!

The interest factor leads to wealth inequality, and the outcome always creates a divide between rich and poor. In the beginning, this may not easily be recognized, but the longer the system runs, the worse it gets. In the end either the currency collapses, or there is a revolution.

Finally, if you think any form of money is the driving force of progress or innovation you are mistaken. Remember, money was primarily invented as a medium of exchange. In ancient time it also was used to store value. What drives change and progress is the creativity and spirit of people combined with the resources of this planet. If you think money is needed in the first place, then that's like saying you need inches to build a house. But precisely that irrational thinking has become the standard and cornerstone of all significant societies!

Likewise the purpose of a business can't be making money, as only banks are allowed by law to make/create money. If a company wants money, it needs to take it from its customers.

Chapter III - From Money to Wealth

Sovereignty - The State of Liberty

„Sovereignty is the full right and power of a governing body over itself, without any interference from outside sources or bodies.“

The word "sovereign" means to be in supreme authority over someone or something and to be extremely effective and powerful. It is usually applied to Gods, royalty, and governments. We speak of kings and queens as sovereigns (even when they are figureheads), and of the sovereign rights of nations and states.

Personal sovereignty, then, would imply the inherent authority and power of an individual to determine his or her direction and destiny. If that sounds suspiciously like free will, it's because personal sovereignty and free will are the same things.[52]

Three institutions are desperately trying - and mostly succeeding - in taking away your sovereignty. These are the banking institution, the government, and the church. The banks take away your freedom to create abundance. They force you into accepting their money, which is then outside of your control. The government takes away your complete rights of what you can and can't do. This process starts with your birth certificate. The moment this is issued your status of being a sovereign being has been taken away and replaced by the rights and rules the government issues. The third institution is the church, which is convincing you that you can't directly connect with a higher power - like God or whatever word you want to use.

- Banks - Replacing Abundance with Scarcity
- Governments - Replacing Power with Laws & Regulations
- Church - Replacing Faith with Sin

Being a sovereign nation means having the right and power to make decisions and take actions in the national interest, without being forced to by another country. Being a sovereign person means being able to choose one's actions without being forced to by another person. To the degree there is free will in all such choices, national or personal, there is sovereignty.

The way to increase your sovereignty is to improve your use of free will. Decide for yourself, what actions to take in any situation. Also decide for yourself how to interpret your actions and responses, whether they are freely chosen or not.

For instance, if you work for someone and ordered to do an unpleasant task, it can feel like you have lost your free will. However, you can always quit, you can also decide for yourself that you are not working for the boss. You are providing a compensated service, and you can do the task because you choose to, not because you are ordered. The point is, you can always choose your actions.

Beware, though. Personal sovereignty has a high price. It's called personal responsibility. As you increase your use of free will, you also increase your responsibility for your actions and reactions. Increase it enough, and you won't be able to blame your parents, your enemies, your friends, your lovers or spouse, government, bad genes, society, fate, Satan or God for anything having to do with your experience.

If a lot of people were to increase their responsibility significantly, our society would undergo tremendous change. Co-dependent and manipulative relationships would all but disappear; most trial lawyers would have to find new professions; politicians would be held accountable for their decisions; insurance companies would have to change their policies; people of different religion would be more tolerant of each other, humanity would act more from love than fear.

Now, what kind of world would that be? [53]

The Shift from Money to Wealth

„The real measure of our wealth is how much we'd be worth if we lost all our money." - John Henry Jowett, British Protestant preacher

Have you ever imagined that the money rabbit hole goes that deep? I doubt that even 1% of the population have the slightest idea how money works.

On the contrary, many people ,sense' - for quite a time now - that things are not going the right way. If they invested considerable time to dig deep into this money hole, they would find nothing else than bits and pieces, conspiracy theories and abstract mathematical economic formulas. As long as people can't see the puzzle as one big picture, they are trying to fix it by applying patchworks in the form of new laws and regulations.

All fixes that have been applied in the past have made things worse!

What you will learn in the next few chapters are not the usual quick fix method's (e.g., changing interest rates, printing more money), which are discussed by various economic and political establishments. To find a real working solution, you must go all the way down into that money rabbit hole, understand the real underlying principles of money, and the most profound concept our society is based. Once you arrive at this helicopter viewpoint, you can see the whole picture and all its connected issues.

There are solutions, so simple and profound that your mind may discard it as absurd or even nonsense. It's understandable because it will question the foundation of your current belief systems. It's the carpet you walk on.

Einstein once said - the solution to a problem cannot be found at the same level of thinking that it created.

So, please bear with me through the next few chapters, and challenge your mind to be open and stay open to understand new ideas and solutions, that may sound crazy at first.

There is nothing more important in life than to stay open to new concepts and beliefs. How could you ever change your life for the better if you stay within your own - or even worse - in someone else's footprints. Your willingness to learn new aspects and viewpoints of life determines the amount of success in your life. Life itself is constant change, and nothing ever stays the same. Laws and rules change, opinions change, conditions change, people change, and thoughts and feelings change.

The idea that life itself is an ongoing, stable and controllable process creates constant friction within yourself.

One of the most solid concepts in our western culture is the belief that each of us lives an entirely independent life. We are all separated from each other, and nature. You will come to see that this concept is one of the leading causes of the mess we have created and that scientific facts prove quite the opposite. What I am going to reveal to you in the next few chapters are nothing else than basic facts, we have either lost in our cultural heritage or just ignored for a long time.

Now, please follow me on a ride through mind-expanding sociological, psychological and spiritual insights. I hope it will shine a new light on how you see money, and how you could free yourself from it. A guided path, which will lead you from illusions to the truth.

Money And Wealth - What's The Difference?

„Wealth - The Conditions of Well Being"

The word wealth comes from the Medieval English word 'weal' and 'th.' 'Weal' means 'well being' and 'th' means 'the condition of.' A better and more authentic definition of wealth, therefore, is 'The Condition of Well Being.' Wealth is what we value most in our lives.

Areas like relationships, environmental conditions and happiness are essential ingredients for our well being and currently wholly left out in the measurement of our well being. If we do not measure all aspects of well being, we will not only ignore these areas we will also fail to improve them.

What we value most about life defines our real wealth.

All factors that contribute to well-being could be called life capital or life assets. It is often said that we too often know the cost of everything and the value of nothing.

Wealth can also be defined from the point of view of these four categories:

- Social Capital
- Cultural Capital
- Natural Capital
- Spiritual Capital

Social capital is the totality of human relationships that sustain life and make it rich. It includes community, friendships, fun, teaching, and a sense of belonging. Together these constitute a cultural inheritance, a treasure passed on from generation to generation in the form of learned skills, customs, and human connections.

Cultural capital refers to the cumulative products of the human mind, including language, art, stories, music, and ideas.

Natural capital refers to the earth itself: the earth's minerals, land, soil, oceans, fresh water, genomes, and biota; everything, that is, that was not created by human beings.

Spiritual Capital is our imagination, creativity, attention span, playfulness, and spontaneity.

Mark Anielski uses 5 categories of wealth to show the different areas.

- Human Wealth
- Social Wealth
- Natural Wealth
- Manufactured Wealth
- Financial Wealth

Human Wealth

Human wealth is people or human resources. Human wealth can be defined as "the knowledge, skills, competencies, capabilities, and other attributes of each individual that facilitates the creation of personal, social, and economic well-being." Human wealth also includes health (e.g., mental, physical, emotional and spiritual) and time (i.e., life energy).

- People (employees, contractors, suppliers)
- Intellectual capital (Educational attainment, Knowledge, Skills)
- Creativity and entrepreneurship
- Capabilities
- Motivation

- Productivity
- Happiness (self-rated)
- Time use balance (work, family, leisure, community)
- Health (disease, diet, overall health)
- Physical well-being (fitness)
- Mental well-being
- Addictions (drugs, alcohol, gambling)
- Workplace safety
- Training and professional development
- Personal self-development

Social Wealth

Social wealth refers to the strength of our relationships with each other and the strength of our interdependence (John McKnight) which would include such things as trust, networks, shared responsibility, reciprocity, neighborliness, and a sense of community. These can also be called our social resources.

- Customer relations (value, loyalty and commitment by customers)
- Supplier relations (value and commitment by suppliers)
- Reputation
- Workplace relationships
- Workplace climate (e.g. stress, comradery, sense of collective commitment)
- Social cohesion (teams and team spirit)
- Workplace climate (happiness with work)
- Equity (incomes, age-sex distribution, women in management)
- Employee family quality of life
- Networks
- Friendships amongst workplace colleagues
- Membership in professional associations, clubs or other organizations
- Social events with colleagues

- Family outings with work place colleagues
- Financial investment/giving/donations to the community

Natural Wealth

Natural wealth or natural resources are nature's goods and services, whether trees, land, water, air or wildlife. Natural capital also includes the ecological services provided by watersheds and wetlands in maintaining clean air and clean water. Natural capital is vital for our economic well-being.

- Environmental goods and services
- Natural capital (stocks and flows)
- Land
- Minerals
- Oil, Gas, Coal
- Forests (Trees)
- Fish and Wildlife
- Water
- Air
- Carbon Sinks
- Ecosystem Integrity
- Energy (by type, source, and end-use)

Manufactured Wealth

Manufactured wealth or manufactured resources are things like equipment, factories, tools and anything physical infrastructure that has been built by investing both human capital (time, labor, ideas) and natural capital (resources). Manufactured wealth contributes to our overall economic well-being by providing the means to a more comfortable and enhanced quality of life.

Manufactured wealth would include both private and public infrastructure - homes, household, appliances, cars, factories, hospitals, schools, and roads. It would also include new technology, designs, patents, processes, and ideas.

- Infrastructure
- Roads
- Pipelines
- Transmission lines
- Other Structures
- Buildings
- Machinery and equipment
- Technology
- Patents
- Brands
- Intellectual property (ideas, innovations)
- Management processes
- Production processes
- Databases

Financial Wealth

Financial wealth or money resources include current money - valued assets - cash, savings, investments, real estate and other money - valuable things. Financial capital also includes debt and financial liabilities.

- Financial Assets (Current financial assets, Cash, Accounts receivable, Inventories)
- Capital assets (Financial Liabilities, Debt (short and long-term borrowings), Accounts payable
- Shareholders' Equity (Preferred securities, Share capital, Retained earnings)

Money or currency is only needed to transfer wealth not to create it. The purpose is to create wealth, not money!

A New Definition of Money

„Wealth is the ability to fully experience life.“ - Henry David Thoreau, American essayist, poet and philosopher

As we experience an increase in global destabilization, we see a massive transfer of wealth going from the poor and middle class to the rich and super-rich.

In 2017 the top 1% controlled 50% of the wealth on this planet!

History shows us that this transfer usually indicates the end of a monetary system and the start of a new one. It gives us the opportunity to disassociate ourselves from the identity of money, and let us again focus on creating wealth. It's no easy task as we likely blame others first - especially the banks. However, it will give us the opportunity to free ourselves again from monetary slavery, and start aligning again with the principles of nature and its inherent state of abundance.

How Do We Measure?

Laws of nature are merely observed regularities in the way things behave. To find rhythms, you must look at things through something regular. You must lay a ruler alongside them, or compare its behavior with the usual functioning of a clock. But clocks and rulers are human inventions. They are regular measures which we use for comparing the rates of change.

A clock measures the rate of change. It's entirely arbitrary, but we very easily compare our regulation measuring devices with what makes things happen. As if the sun rises because it's 6 o'clock in the morning.[54]

Brilliant and creative people have invented math and with it all forms of measurements to make our life easier. We have watches that measure time. It makes catching a bus simple. No need to stand around for hours – waiting and guessing when one will arrive.

The same is true for the measurement of inches and feet, which measure length. An inch is defined as a unit of linear measure equal to one-twelfth of a foot or 2.54 cm. A foot has been determined by international agreement as equivalent to 0.3048 meters accurately. We can construct machines, build houses and invent great things without continually agreeing on measurements. We usually never think about this – it's a given.

What would happen if someone manipulates these measurements all the time? One day an inch would be 5% more than the day before, stay for a month and then goes back 5% to its original value. Then six months later it would go to 5% less.

It would cause massive chaos, confusion, and problems for all people using this particular measurement. People using it would quickly abandon it and look for something more stable. Or they would come together and put effort into it to stabilize it. This example of length as a particular measurement is easy to understand.

Money Measures Value

Another form of measurement is money. To exchange and do business, we invented money, just as we did with time and length. Money puts a value on any service or physical object to trade it. Money is the measurement that makes it possible to compare and convert goods and services with each other.

The value of anything in the world is usually expressed by how it serves its ecosystem - the goal of making money with a business. It's very artificial and leads to the dangerous thinking of seeing it as a product. What value has a tree, a river or your liver? In truth, no cost can ever be attached to it!

Goods and services represent value to us, and money puts a number on it – it can then be exchanged easily. Money is only necessary for the process of exchange.

Money also became at one point in history the storage of value, but that's another subject. Let's stick for now with the primary purpose of making goods and service exchangeable. You no longer have to carry around a pig to exchange it into a rug, two chickens and a bunch of carrots.

But somewhere down the road, we have started to mistaken the goods and services with money. We are now more interested in the measurement itself than the value it measures. That's being entirely backward in one's thinking, and we get into the same confusion when we imagine, for example, that money represents wealth.

It's like saying you are more interested in time rather than what you can do with time. It's like talking about the sunset, but missing the experience of it. This ingrained thinking, which happened over a long time, and which is also re-programmed continuously on a daily basis through our money behavior. It's so strong that it is almost transparent to our mind. It's like the window you look through all the time, but you can't see it.

Here is an interesting metaphor from Alan Watts in the form of a story, which illustrates that even further:

There is a man that hired a contractor to build a house. Every other day he goes to the job site and checks on the progress. As usual, he takes a look around and observes the scene. He sees building material lying around and workers that use these building materials to build the house. Occasionally he talks with the contractor itself to get a report of the progress. This is going on for a few weeks. He checks in at the job site, talks to the contractor, and leaves.

One day he gets to the job site, and the workers are sitting on the building materials and gaze into the sky. He checks his clock once again to make sure it's not lunchtime. He also checks if this may be a holiday, but then the workers wouldn't be there in the first place. Strange, what's happening here? He approaches the contractor and asks him why the people are not working. The contractor tells him: „We were running out of inches." Get it?

's precisely how we deal with money. Without money, we don't work. It's insane, but 's so ingrained into our thinking that you may think this is absurd. It shows you how ır we steered away from the natural process of creating value and exchanging services.

.ll the requirements to build the house are in place. There is creativity, the work force, nd there is the building material. Nothing else is needed!

's a false assumption that we need money to produce goods and create services. Mon-y is not needed for it at all. There are still a few cultures on this planet that live entirely ′ithout any form of money. They accomplish all that they need and live a good life - :uly an experience in abundance. We have been told that these cultures are primitive nd uncivilized. If you ever have a chance to observe them and compare their living to urs, you may conclude that their way of life is much saner than ours in the western ′orld.

here is a tremendous amount of wealth in the form of creativity and resources. We ave the technological possibility to create abundance for everyone on earth. As long s we believe that we need money for it, we can't accomplish it.

Prosperity Arrives From Creativity and Resources

"No nation has ever taxed itself into prosperity." - Rush Limbaugh, American radio talk show host

The origin of the word prosperity is middle English: from Old French 'prosperite', from Latin 'prosperitas', from 'prosperous' meaning 'doing well'. Doing well arrives from being well, and that is a state of mind.

We think money makes prosperity, and it's the other way around. It's material prosperity which has money as a way of measuring it. We usually think money has to come from somewhere like hydroelectric power or lumber or iron, and it doesn't. [55]

Money is a measurement we have invented, like inches or seconds.

Whenever there is a depression, what is causing it? Money. There are no less wealth, no less energy, no less raw materials than there were before, but it's like the story with the house. Sorry, you can't build this house today, no inches.

We can have depression because we have no inches to go around or no dollars. That's all a lot of nonsense. We are used to thinking backward, making the metaphysical tail wag the dog. Making the law rule things, whereas it doesn't. It's merely a way of measuring what happens.

Just imagine you would replace the word money with inches in these sentences:

- I have to make more money (inches)
- I am investing in money (inches)

How can you possibly do this? It makes no sense – it's nonsense.

Money is the primary aspect of our physical life. We use it many times on a daily basis, and we don't know what it is. It becomes obvious when the majority of people use something on a regular basis, which they don't understand, the outcome is probably not always what they intended.

It is also apparent if the majority of people do not understand what money is, they become highly influenceable to any suggestions of what others tell them what it is. They can be easily targeted to think and believe it to be something. It is an easy subject to manipulation and mind control.

That's the reason why only a handful of people control major economic decisions and the majority of resources on this planet. If the majority of people would understand the mechanics of money, they would immediately start to make different choices in their lives, and nobody would be able to control them any longer.

Economic growth as we define it today, and money as we describe it today, is part of a story of the people that are becoming obsolete.

The Trouble with GDP

Despite what the GDP (Gross domestic product) statistics say, it's not the creation of new wealth. Instead, it's the conversion of existing wealth into money. We have converted nature into commodities and relationships into services.

Charles Eisenstein writes in his book „Sacred Economics" that from time to time throughout modern history, our ability to do this has reached a temporary impasse. Whenever that happens, a Marxian crisis of capital looms falling returns on capital investment (falling profit margins), falling real wages, transfer of investment into financial speculation, rising indebtedness, and so on in a self-reinforcing circle of misery that can only end in systemic collapse. [56]

Today, the impasse in our ability to convert nature into commodities and relationships into services is not temporary. There is little more we can convert.

The story that is ending in our time, then, goes much deeper than the story of money. It is a story of endless growth, and the money system we have today is an embodiment of that story, enabling and propelling the conversion of the natural realm into the human domain.

It began millennia ago when humans first tamed fire and made tools; it accelerated when we applied these tools to the domestication of animals and plants, and began to conquer the wild, to make the world ours. It reached its glorious zenith in the age of the machine, when we created a wholly artificial world, harnessing all the forces of nature and imagining ourselves to be its lords and possessors. And now, that story is drawing to a close, as the inexorable realization dawns that the story is not true.

Despite our pretenses, the world is not ours; despite our illusions, we are not in control of it. As the unintended consequences of technology proliferate, as our communities, our health, and the ecological basis of civilization deteriorate, as we explore new depths of misery, violence, and alienation, we enter the final stages of a story nearing completion: crisis, climax, and denouement.

It is time, therefore, to enter into a new story and a new kind of money that embodies it. Just as life does not end with adolescence, neither does civilization's evolution stop with the end of growth. We are in the midst of a transition parallel to an adolescent's transition into adulthood.

Physical growth ceases, and ones vital resources turn inward to foster growth in other realms. In childhood, it is right for a person to do what is necessary to grow, both physically and mentally. A good mother provides the resources for this growth, as our Mother Earth has done for us.

An infant does not have a strong self-other distinction but takes time to form an identity and an ego and to learn that the world is not an extension of the self. So it has been for humanity collectively. [57]

But as the extreme of yang contains the birth of yin, so does the extreme of separation include the seed of what comes next: reunion. Because in adolescence, you fall in love, and your world of perfect reason and perfect selfishness falls apart as the self expands to include the beloved within its bounds.

Fully individuated from the Other, you can fall in love with it, and experience a reunion greater than the original union, for it contains within it the entire journey of separation. The environmental movement and numerous spiritual movements are all evidence that we are falling in love again with planet earth.

From this perspective, it is evident that a money system that compels continued physical growth, that forces taking more and more from the earth, is obsolete. It is incompatible with love, with the reunion.

That is why no financial or economic reform can work that does not include a new kind of money. The new money must embody a new story, one that treats nature not as a mother but as a lover. We will still have a need for money for a long time to come, because we need magical symbols to reify our Story of the People, to apply it to the physical world as a creative template.

The essential character of money will not change: it will consist of magical talismans, whether physical or electronic, through which we assign roles, focus intention, and coordinate human activity.

Today's usury-money is part of a story of separation, in which "more for me is less for you." That is the essence of interest: I will only "share" money with you if I end up with even more of it in return.

On the systemic level as well, interest on money creates competition, anxiety, and the polarization of wealth. Meanwhile, the phrase "more for me is less for you" is also the motto of the ego, and a truism was given the discrete and separate self of modern economics, biology, and philosophy.

Only when our sense-of-self expands to include others, through the process called love, is that truism replaced by its opposite: "More for you is also more for me." However, to merely understand and agree with these teachings is not enough; many of us walk around with a divide between what we believe and what we live.

The Birth of a new Story

An actual transformation in the way we experience being is necessary, and such a transformation usually comes about in much the same way as our collective change is happening now: through a collapse of the old story of self and world, and the birth of a new one. For the self, too, is ultimately a story, with a beginning and an end. Have you ever gone through an experience that leaves you, afterward, hardly knowing who you are?

It is also a good description of an economy based on demurrage currency - money that, like all things of nature, decays with time. Demurrage currency contributes to a very different story of the people, of the self, and of the world than usury-money.

It is cyclical, rather than exponential, always returning to its source; it redefines wealth as a function of one's generosity and not one's accumulation; it is the manifestation of abundance, not scarcity. It has the potential to recreate the gift dynamics of primitive societies on a global scale, bringing forth personal gifts and directing them toward human needs.

It nullifies the discounting of future cash flows that enable us to destroy the future for the sake of the present: under demurrage, the best business decision is the best ecological decision and the best social decision. It is thus a currency of sustainability. Because it is not compelled to grow over time, neither does it drag more and more of the world into the realm of commodities and services.

Expressing Your Gifts & Talents

A little reflection reveals that no one can be fulfilled without the opportunity to give fully of her gifts. What makes a job unfulfilling? No matter how highly paid, if you lack the opportunity to apply your gifts toward a purpose that fully inspires you, any job eventually becomes soul-destroying. We are here to express our gifts; it is among our deepest desires, and we cannot be fully alive otherwise.

Here are a few examples: a starry night sky free of light pollution; a countryside free of road noise; a vibrant multi-cultural local urban economy; unpolluted lakes, rivers, and seas; the ecological basis of human civilization. Many of us have gifts that would contribute to all of these things, yet no one will pay us to give them. That's because money as we know it ultimately rests on converting the public into the private. The new money will encourage the opposite, and the conflict between our ideals and practical financial reality will end.

The era of taking is over. The new era of giving has already begun.

Usury-money (based on Interest) is the money of growth, and it was perfect for humanity's growth stage on earth, and for the story of ascent, dominance, and mastery. The next step is one of co-creative partnership with earth. The Story of the People for this new stage is coming together right now.

Its weavers are the visionaries of fields like permaculture, holistic medicine, renewable energy, mycoremediation, local currencies, restorative justice, attachment parenting, and a million more.

To undo the damage that the ‚Age of Usury' has wrought on nature, culture, health, and spirit will require all the gifts that make us human, and indeed is so impossibly demanding that it will take those gifts to a new level of development.

Just as usury-money has mobilized humanity's gifts for the purposes of growth and domination, the new money will mobilize them for healing and beauty. Because money will not be under compulsion to grow, no longer will art be under compulsion to sell itself.

Today, any endeavor that does not involve an expansion of the realm of monetized goods and services must go against the economic current. Such is the character of exponential money. But cyclical money has a different character: anything that violates nature's law "Waste is food" will go against the economic current. The division between work and art will disappear, and it will no longer be possible to be a sellout. The conflict between our idealism and economic necessity will vanish.

As the truth of that sinks in, deeper and deeper, and as the convergence of crises pushes us out of the old world, more and more people will live from that truth. The truth that more for you is not less for me; the truth that what I do unto you, so I do unto myself; the truth of living to give what you can and take what you need.

We can start doing it right now. We are afraid, but when we do it for real, the world meets our needs and more. We then find that the story of „Separation", embodied in the money we have known, is not true and never was. Yet, the last ten millennia were not in vain.

Sometimes it is necessary to live a lie to its fullest before we are ready to take the next step into the truth. The lie of separation in the age of usury is now complete. We have explored its fullness, its furthest extremes, and seen all it has wrought, the deserts and the prisons, the concentration camps and the wars, the wastage of the good, the true, and the beautiful.

Money in the Golden Age

„The key to abundance is meeting limited circumstances with unlim- ited thoughts." - Marianne Williamson, American spiritual teacher, author, and lecturer

Early forms of commodity-money, such as grain, cattle, and the like were undoubtedly subject to decay: grain spoils, cattle age and die, and even farmland reverts to wilderness if left untended. There have also been metallic money systems that approximated the phenomenon of decay by incorporating a kind of built-in negative interest rate. [58]

A crude example of such a system was in extensive use in the Middle Ages in Europe's 'bracteates' system, in which coins were periodically recalled and then re-minted at a discount rate. In the period from 1150 to 1450 - about three hundred years - in a part of today's Germany existed this 'bracteates' system of money. This time has also been called the 'golden age,' a very happy time. The saying "craft has golden ground" ought to have its origins from this time.

People lived a whole 300 years without money worries and work pressure.

At the beginning of the Middle Ages, it was customary to collect the coins when the ruler of the country changed. They were then melted and re-shaped and handed out again to the public.

Around 1150 Archbishop Wichmann from Magdeburg began to issue coins which were called in twice a year for exchange. The aim was to collect taxes easily and regularly. 12 old pennies were replaced with nine new, and the difference was collected tax.

To melt the coins quickly, and re-stamp them without much hassle, the domination was only on one side and made of thin sheet metal. That's how this money also became its name, as 'Bracteates' means a thin sheet of metal. Soon, this method spread all over the country.

This meant that hoarding was no longer profitable. To escape the next exchange, money was lent without interest, because only the owner of the coins had to pay the exchange fee. Again, money was a pure medium of exchange, and no longer a treasure to keep.

It resulted in the most magnificent development period in German history.

The money was exchanged in a certain rhythm, and with every exchange a specific fee was payable. The bracteates circulated much faster than our present money, up to 52 times. Because of the reduction, which is nothing else than a negative interest rate, everyone wanted to get rid of the money as soon as possible to escape the deflation.

To save the fees, the money could be lent interest-free. Only the current owner had the obligation to pay fees, and also the lender benefited because the interest was waived.

Because of the obligation to pay fees, it slowly became annoying to have money, and it was therefore used for extensive investment. It resulted in a big boom in craft and art. It was at this time where many beautiful cathedrals were built, and also the development of Gothic. Because of the prevailing general prosperity, these buildings often arose from voluntary donations by citizens who could afford it. Most major cities were founded during this booming economic time. By 1450, as the interest of money was reintroduced, the so-called 'Dark Ages' started.

The Medieval age is mostly associated with negative perceptions of oppression and servitude. Hardly anyone noticed that this time had a golden age well as dark period. The golden age is represented by the Gothic and can be limited to the period between 1150-1450.

At that time social differences were as balanced as never in the course of history. People gained prosperity through work, not through the effect of effortless interest rates. The minimum non-working days per year was 90, often above 150! Very soon the Monday was introduced as a day off as well, and craftsmen were working in the week only four days. The income was so high that in Augsburg a day laborer with his daily earnings could afford 5-6 pounds of expensive meat every day.

From these descriptions emerges that there was no exploitation of labor power and pressure, as is often claimed. People did not live at that time to work, but they worked to live.

The development of all major cities in Germany demonstrates how great this economic boom must have been. This example also shows that there was no economic downturns or economic crises in this particular period.

In England, Saxon kings re-coined silver pennies every six years, issuing three for every four taken in, for a depreciation rate of about 4 percent per year. This effectively imposed a penalty on the hoarding of money, encouraging its circulation and investment in productive capital instead.

If you had more money than you could use, you would be happy to lend it, even at zero interest, because your coins would decrease in value if you held them too long. Note that the money supply didn't necessarily shrink as a result of this system since the lord would presumably inject the difference back into the economy to cover his expenses. This negative interest on money was thus a kind of a tax.

The Austrian Example

The depressed town of Wörgl, Austria, issued its own stamp money. The Wörgl currency was by all accounts a huge success. Roads were paved, bridges built, and back taxes were paid. The unemployment rate plummeted, and the economy thrived, attracting the attention of nearby towns. Mayors and officials from all over the world began to visit Wörgl until, as in Germany, the central government abolished the Wörgl currency and the town slipped back into depression.

The Wörgl currency contained a demurrage rate of 1 percent per month. Contemporary accounts attributed to this the very rapid velocity of the currencies circulation. Instead of generating interest and growing, accumulation of money became a burden, much like possessions are a burden to the nomadic hunter-gatherer.

The Free Money System

Make no mistake: the consequences of a free-money system would be profound, encompassing economic, social, psychological, and spiritual dimensions. Money is so fundamental, so defining of our civilization that it would be naive to hope for any authentic civilizational shift that did not involve a significant change in money as well.

Official economic statistics have hidden the probability that the Western economies have been in a zero-growth phase for at least twenty years. Whatever growth there has been, mainly come from such things as real estate bubbles, the prison industry, health care costs, insurance and financial services, educational costs, the weapons industry, and so forth.

The more expensive these are, the more the economy is assumed to have grown. In areas where there has been growth, such as the Internet, much of this is a covert form of importing growth. Internet-based revenue comes mostly from sales and advertising, not from new production.

What is the economic value of companies like Facebook and Twitter?

We are more efficiently greasing the wheels of the conveyor belt of goods from China to the West. In any event, developing countries cannot keep the growth machine running forever. The more it slows, the more it will be necessary to get around the zero bound. [59]

You are not creating value or any form of wealth by making money from money. You are talking away money from a natural process of free flow, where it would go naturally, and where it's the most needed. For most people that's such a harsh change in perspective, it takes a lot of willingness and open-mindedness to learn to see this viewpoint.

Money has come a long way and has gone through varies cycles of how it is defined and how it is used. We are currently in the stage of a cycle, where we see that the model and functionality of money leads to more limitation than freedom.

History shows that individual countries had gone through similar stages before. However, never before in history did we have one global economic system. No longer is the Chinese or Japanese economy separated from the European or the American. It's all interwoven as you can see in the stock markets.

From Liabilities to Creating Assets

"Time, not money, is your biggest asset in life. You need time to invest in relationships (with yourself and your family) or to chase your passion. Think again if you are still trading off time for money. Let your money work for you. You don't work for money. That is exactly what Financial Freedom is..." - Manoj Arora, Indian best seller author

It is easy to confuse assets and liabilities, but the two are actually the opposite of one another. Any item that you purchase will fall under one of the two categories. All products you buy have a cost beyond the price of the item itself.

What is an Asset?

An asset is an investment that brings in money on a consistent basis. Such earning assets create revenue streams directly because you either own them or you control them. More than just a representation of value, a real asset is one that will generate money for you. Assets bring in money without requiring that you work to earn money. Retirement plans and investments, for example, are both assets.

They contribute to a steady stream of income, which you can use to cover your living expenses in your retirement or to increase your cash flow. Once you have invested in these assets, they usually become a consistent income stream. That's basically what wealthy people do.

What is a Liability?

Liabilities usually represent obligations that you have. A debt that you have not paid is always a liability, even if you own something against it, like a house or a car. Liabilities can be short term or long term.

Debts that you will pay off in under a year are considered to be short-term liabilities. Debts that you will pay off in a time frame of over a few years, such as a car payment or mortgage, are long-term liabilities. There are many examples of liabilities in debts that you owe. Lines of credit, mortgages, second mortgages, car payments, and liens of all types are each liabilities.

A liability is also an item that costs you money or takes money away from you. A house that you owe money on is a liability and not an asset. A boat, for which you make payments falls under the category of liability as well. Even a boat that you have paid for is a liability as it will cost you significant money every month in maintenance, upkeep, and dock fees.

The definition of liability can also be extended to things you buy that only cost you money upfront. Even though a flat screen television may not cost you money every month to own, it presents an opportunity cost.

The opportunity cost is the money you may have invested in an asset and is now lost. With the money that you spend on the television, you could have instead purchased an investment that brings in money to you on a regular basis. All investments that provide you with steady income would count as assets.

The flat screen television takes money away from you because it loses value and does not bring any money back to you - it is a liability.

Liabilities Distract You From Creating Assets

Liabilities also distract you and keep your focus away from creating assets that bring in money. When you always think of how you will pay your mortgage payment, car payment, and other bills, it saps your energy and consumes your free attention. Every liability takes your focus away from developing assets.

Few things can cause a more significant distraction than endless hours spent in front of the TV. A time you could instead use to start an e-commerce site, develop a side business, teach yourself a new skill, or learn how to invest in valuable assets.

The Real Cost of Liabilities

Assume for a moment that you purchase a television for $1,000. In a few years that TV is maybe worth $200. You sell it and buy the latest version for now maybe $800. In a few years, you lost already about $1400. Some people buy a new television set every five years! Can you calculate what that loss amounts to in 40-50 years?

If you invest instead the $1,000 into a high yield investment that pays 15% percent each year, then you will receive $150 each year in additional income.

That may not sound like much at first but think about these returns over five years. Now we are talking about $150 x 5 equals $750. Your original $1,000 would soon have been increased to $1,750, that's almost double the amount of the beginning.

None of these examples assume that you reinvest the gains each year. For example, in the second year, you could reinvest your $150 profits from the first year and have now $1,150 to earn returns on the next year. Following this example, at the end of the second year, you would have already $1,322.50. It's the power of compounding interest! By the end of five years, this would bring you up to $2,313.50. At the end of ten years, you would have $4,652.34.

Compound interest is the addition of interest to the principal sum of a loan or deposit, or in other words, interest on interest. It is the result of reinvesting interest, rather than paying it out, so that interest in the next period is then earned on the principal sum plus previously accumulated interest.[60]

Over the time span of 20 years, your total investment would have grown through continually reinvesting the returns to a staggering amount of over $12,000. How much does that appealing $1,000 television costs you when you calculate the lost opportunity cost?

Wealthy people invest first in assets and buy later their liabilities - if any - from the earnings of these assets. They think about serving others first, which works like wonders.

Wealthy people have some more tricks up their sleeves. They usually secure the money they earn from assets with a trust fund. Their children and the generation after them inherit this trust fund. When they need money, they borrow it from their trust fund and pay themselves interest on what they borrow! This is a remarkable concept, not to be mistaken with the life insurance concept „bank on yourself." It ensures the trust fund is continuously growing over time due to an inflow of money from assets as well as interest payments from loans.

Overcome the Urge of Instant Gratification

Are you looking for the next get rich quick scheme? Do you play the lottery? Do you frequently watch videos or attend online webinars that promise how to get rich overnight, instead of learning sound business techniques that you can apply to build your successful carrier?

Do you believe that faster is always better, and slow is inefficient? We live in the fast lane, enjoy fast food, demand fast service, and expect results almost instantly. We want all of it - right now!

Some people argue that technology is responsible for this instant gratification syndrome. Technology offers a way to do more in less time. We can communicate with almost any person on the planet, at any given time, instantly through texting, e-mail, cell phones, and social networks like Twitter and Facebook.

The industry is exploiting our immediate gratification demand. We are not only inundated by billboards on every highway but also beaten with advertising on every website we visit. Each message tries to stimulate us toward the impulse buy. Instant gratification has also affected our entire monetary system.

You may live your life with an instant gratification habit, and not aware of how it's affecting your wealth. You probably buy impulsively much more than you think. Start to keep track of what you purchase for at least a thirty-day period. Then take a look and highlight any frivolous spending you find. Add up all the frivolous spending and think about what effect it would have over a period of one year if you would put it in a savings account or use it to pay down debt.

Get into the mindset of asking yourself: 'Do I want this or do I need this?' before making any purchase at all. After a little practice, it will become second nature. The more you are going to spend on a single acquisition the longer you should think about it. Get out of the trap that bargains only last for a short moment, and you have to buy immediately. You will be surprised how much extra money you have left in the bank at month end if you practice this approach.

It may sound elementary, but the only way to get control of your finances is to save more, spend less, avoid liabilities, and bad debt. You need to manage your money behavior before you see a positive change in your finances.

Pick up a copy of „Rich Dad Poor Dad" by Robert Kiyosaki. It advocates the importance of financial literacy, financial independence and building wealth through investing in assets.[61]

From Seeking a Job to Finding Your True Calling

"Before I can tell my life what I want to do with it, I must listen to my life telling me who I am." - Parker J. Palmer, Author, educator, and activist

A job is something you are seeking outside of yourself. It's a mindset that originates from the belief that there is a limited amount of possibilities to make money. It's the assumption that there specific categories, where you have to fit in. It is the conclusion you make that you have to match one of those limited job categories. It's already a challenging task, and it will get even more difficult in the future.

A job means you trade your time for money and immediately, the "Fairness Game" comes in.

- How can I get the job and not the other?
- Do I get paid enough?
- Who gets paid more then me?
- What can I do to get a promotion?

Fairness is an energy sucker. It takes time, consumes energy and prevents collaboration. It's inefficient as everybody has a personal opinion about what fairness is.

The indoctrination starts in early childhood with the question: "What do you want to become when you are a grown up?" It already implies that you can't stay with who you are, with your intrinsic values, gifts and talents that have been given to you since day one. You have to become someone else – how confusing. You have to leave your artistic heritage behind and learn to become someone else, that fits the profile of the economic structure.

The current school system confuses the students, one sees and hears something, only to forget it later again. It teaches to accept class affiliation, makes them indifferent, emotionally and intellectually dependent. It shows an illusionary self-confidence, which requires the constant confirmation by experts to keep this false illusionary self-confidence alive. It lays the foundation of a competing attitude, which leads to stress, early exhaustion and later adulthood that is driven by fear and scarcity.

I will never forget the words carved in on my wooden school desk: „Right here a genius becomes a zombie".

The topics and methods that are taught today are entirely outdated and provide skills for jobs that won't exist any longer after school is finished. It is based on an old model that was fitting the job requirements of the industrial revolution.

By the way, when did we start using the name job instead of work?

The dictionary's first explanation is: 'a piece of work, especially a specific task done as part of the routine of one's occupation or for an agreed price.'

The definition of ‚jobs' already implies that they are temporary. Work has shopped down to become a task. It used to be a life's assignment, and now it's split into short-term economic snippets. It has been downgraded to a soul-less, meaningless transaction. Your time in exchange for money. That's where the phrase 'time is money' originates.

The Only Reason to Get a Job

If you do a job - don't do it for the sake of money. Do it because you want to learn what there is to learn from it. When there is nothing more to gain from it – move on. If you continue to do the job for the money you are stuck forever in 'the rat race,' and you stop evolving.

What Is Your Calling?

A calling is a recognition inside yourself. It is the awareness and perception that arises from the unique gifts and talents you came into this world. It's the thrive you feel to do something with what you are passioned. It's the natural way of life to express and succeed itself through you. Using your gifts and talents to contribute to the overall improvement, and ultimately maintaining the state of lasting abundance.

Abundance thrives evolution.

What Do You Really Desire?

What would you like to do if money were no object? How would you enjoy spending your life? Maybe become a painter, a poet or a writer? Perhaps you would like to live in the wilderness and ride horses, or you may want to teach in an art school?

What do you want to do with your life?

If you think money is the most important thing, you will waste your life. You'll do things you don't like to justify making a living. That is, to go on doing things you don't like doing, which is a state of mental disorder.

Isn't it better to have a short life that is full of what you like doing than a long life spent miserable?

If you like what you're doing, in time, you eventually become a master of it. The only way to become a master of something is to be passionate about it, further study it, continue to practice it, and as a result, you'll be able to get a reasonable fee.

It's a life wasted spending time doing things you don't like, and to teach your children to follow in the same track. We are bringing up children and educating them to live the same sort of lives we're living, but do not realize that times and conditions have dramatically changed.

Therefore, it's essential to consider the question: What do I desire? You've always been looking for something, that something that sets you apart. That something that makes you more than the person you're living as, more into the person you were created to be. What others see as mundane, you see as magnificent. You catch a glimpse of something new, and it becomes something significant.

It's that something extra that keeps you up at night. The hours pass by while everyone else sleeps. You dream, you imagine, you envision what your life might be.

What if you were born for more? There's got to be more than just this. You want to be used, that's your greatest wish. The demand for you has always been genuine. You are gifted and passionate. It's the purpose of life to bring out the most brilliant gifts and talents in you - if you allow it to happen.

- What will you do with what you've been given?
- Will you put it into motion?
- Will you take on the responsibility?

Will you follow ‚the calling' that has been placed into your life? To be fulfilled? To be engaged? To cast out all fears, doubts, and uncertainties To stand strong. To rise, to become who you were created to be. [62]

From Sales to Service

There is a spiritual aspect to our lives – when we give, we receive – when a business does something good for somebody, that somebody feels good about them! – Ben Cohen, American businessman, activist, and philanthropist

Sales used to be to serve someone's need. In the old days of commerce, every transaction was fulfilling a need and was matched with a service in the form of a product. The emphasis was on satisfying a demand from a person. At that time people would not name their business partners customers. This name was coined later during the industrial revolution with the beginning of producing products in mass quantity.

Maybe you remember the old saying: 'The customer is king' and 'The customer is always right.' Even at that time of mass production, the focus was entirely on customer satisfaction. Since a few decades now, we have drifted far away from that attitude and the viewpoint has changed from service to sales. But we have also reached the near end of this sales attitude and seeing slowly the beginning of a new trend of getting back to service.

With the beginning of the industrial revolution machines almost exploded production time. Where you had one person before doing one task, the machine would not only multiply that task, do it faster, but also would no longer need a lunch or coffee break.

This lead to products that the mass could afford. At the turn of the century, a car was a luxury product that only the very rich could afford. With the invention of the assembly line by Henry Ford, the mass production of vehicles was made possible.

Over a time span of 20 years, the famous T-Model was produced. Every year it was produced cheaper by optimizing the production process. Henry Ford was obsessed and driven by this optimization process. Did you know that he tried to build cars before inventing the assembly line? He failed miserably and finally gave up and concentrated his energy on the sole purpose of optimizing the production.

Every year the advantage of optimization was priced into the car, and every year it was sold at a lower price. At the peak of the T-Model, it had a market share of 30 percent. It was so cheap, all of the workers could afford and drive one.

Products could now be produced at a much lower cost and were suddenly available to a much bigger market - the middle class. The people who worked in the factories and fabrics. These were the times when the United States saw it's most significant economic expansion. Productivity was going through the roof.

Meanwhile, with the power of the Internet and the vast advantage of intelligent computer networks, advertising for businesses became a scientific approach. The tracking of every move you make, every product you buy, and every comment you make are analyzed and computed into an individual customer profile.

If you use Facebook, Twitter, and other social networks, then you give away valuable information to advertising companies in exchange for using these services. These vast social networks have become massive customer profiling operations. They collect billions of individual data pieces and combine them to perfect customized, individualized profiles, which advertising companies use to sell you more stuff.

Very advanced and sophisticated mathematical models are now invented by artificially intelligent computer algorithms and combined with large physiological, behavioral studies to sell you even more.

This insane thinking – entirely based on controlling the customer – not only leads to an excess of useless products we don't need, it also creates products designed to break down faster and more often.

The Custom of Bargaining

If you have ever traveled to countries like India, Thailand or the Philippines, you may observe that prices on goods and services are negotiable. Often products don't even show a price label. You ask for the price, and the bargain with the person starts. A very uncommon practice for people in the western world. From our viewpoint, it's a waste of time. Just take my money so I can move on.

The custom of bargaining is a way to get in contact, to establish a relationship, to talk to each other. It's not about the final price that you pay. It's about the connection between two people in the first place.

When Steve Jobs was working on the McIntosh computer, he had catapulted Apple's success to a new dimension. However, soon after 1984 sales went sharply down and Apple was in one of its biggest crises. At that point, Steve Jobs approached the marketing head of Pepsi – at that time – John Sculley. Steve said to him: 'Do you want to sell sugar water for the rest of your life, or do you want to come with me and change the world?' John Sculley turned Pepsi into a world brand.

The Focus on Sales is a Disconnect from Relationship

If the primary focus is on selling, it disconnects you from being in touch with what you sell. The product or service you sell becomes irrelevant to the question if it is ethical, helps people, is it good for the environment, or creates a better world.

The approach of selling misses its purpose. A sale reflects a transaction that arises from excellent customer service. We have it all backward! It's the same with money. We think we need money first, and then we can do something with it to create wealth.

It's all entirely upside down. You first create wealth, and as a result, people use it and share it. Only if you have products and services, will you able to transfer them temporarily into money to trade it.

Look further down the road. The primary focus on sales will lead to more control and manipulation. At the end of the road, none of our freedom will be left. Everything will be controlled and manipulated. It's a human-made model that is not compatible with life, and the inherent principles of nature. Nature is a self-organizing and self-correcting system. It has built-in feedback loops that ensure it stays in perfect equilibrium, healthy and all parts are fulfilling their purpose to its best ability. This feedback loop does not exist with a top to down model of control and manipulation.

One of the primary principles and inherent thrives of life is the expansion of freedom. The freedom to move and expand into new areas and explore new territory. A few hundred years ago humankind was not able to dive into oceans, to swim for hours underwater, or to fly and to go into space. Look back a few million years, and you see evolution was always driving towards greater freedom. The industrial revolution was the beginning of using our minds in a profound new way. It was the beginning to replace workers with machines.

We now start realizing we got sold out on the way. We have become dollar breeding slaves. Our freedom is shrinking instead of expanding. We now have all the machines to help or even eliminate our workload, but we work more, and stress has become standard. We are slowly approaching the end of the rope.

With the mindset of selling we no longer see the other as a person, we see them as an opportunity to make a transaction. The person becomes irrelevant, and the deals become the primary focus. However, to establish and maintain relationships between people is an essential building block to create wealth.

ll Relationships Are Spiritual Assignments

ll relationships are spiritual assignments, that help us see who we really are. Other eople mirror and reflect shades of us we are usually not able to see as part of ourselves. hey help us grow, expand and fulfill our purpose of life by illuminating our mind to ew levels.

elling products is not your purpose in life.

/hen you understand that relationships help and support you in becoming who you e, and fulfilling your highest potential, you can't any longer focus on selling. Selling isses the point entirely, and it bypasses the opportunity. It will make you feel empty id lonely, isolated and soon depressed. Your heart and soul is missing a crucial part of s life force.

nowing that the purpose of every relationship is the empowerment of its people, your itire focus should then become the empowerment of others. By empowering others ju act on this archetype of nature, and by doing so, it will empower you. It's in your iterest to do it, and it has nothing to do with giving first and then receiving. It is based n sharing your gifts and talents, and in doing so, it empowers you first and then the ther as well. You don't seek out to find your power, you find it by using it.

eople will feel good in your presence. When they come into your home or store, they in sense your good intention, and they stick around. They may not consciously know hy, but they somehow feel welcome. What better foundation can there be to start uilding a relationship. When people around you and your business feel good, they pproach you from openness and trust. You immediately have a connection with them. here is no longer a need to convince the person, no need to contact them - they come) you.

was once reading a study, in which people gave a different meaning to relationships, epending on whether they live in the western world or in Asian countries. Most of the estern people focus on what they can get out of a relationship. For the Asian people, it's just the opposite. They focus on what they can bring into a relationship. It's obvious that both points of view create a different reality!

Being of Service

Being of service is the highest form of living your potential. It is your essential and natural purpose to do so. Your energetic and gene blueprint is set up for you with individual abilities, talents, and gifts. By growing from a cell to an adult these gifts and talent are ready to be shared. Like a flower that is ready to bloom and spread its nectar, the bees will come.

Your purpose on earth is to bring your genetic and energetic blueprint into physical reality. You do this by following your passion, which is usually first perceived as your challenge. Once you are willing to face and accept your challenges, you discover your potential. Using this potential will lead to the fulfillment and the true destiny of your life. You become a vessel of service by allowing your talents and gifts to flourish in its natural way. Life intends to support and empower you in every moment you get there.

Don't worry if you get lost on your way as long as you take breaks to realign with your self. Your Life's path is like a GPS, programmed with its destination. When you make ,wrong' turn, it will re-calculate the route to its former destination - always!

From Transactions to Relations

"You can make more friends in two months by becoming interested in other people than you can in two years by trying to get other people interested in you." - Dale Carnegie, American writer and lecturer

In my late twenties, I visited India and stayed two weeks in Bombay. On one of my outings, I attended a small store on the edge of town. I noticed a chess board with its figures sitting at the bottom of the window. It was a beautifully handcrafted board, and I wanted to bring it home as a present. Asking the man in the store about the price he replied: „What do you want to pay?" I was a bit confused and asked him again what it costs. I got the same answer. People told me that bargaining is a tradition in India, so I went ahead and started by giving him a low number. He immediately changed the subject and asked me from which country I was. The conversation lasted about 30 minutes - no mention about the chess board at any time.

I ended up not buying the chess board, but I had a fabulous, almost intimate conversation with this man. Point of this story? The purchase does not start with the transaction. It begins with relating to each other. The outcome may be a transaction, but foremost it's about the people. It used to be like that a long time ago.

Not so long ago families owned small stores. Upon entering the store, a friendly, familiar person would greed you. Someone you knew since the first time you shopped there. If that person were missing one day, you would care about its whereabouts? Would you miss the social interaction?

These days we go to Walmart, Costco and all the other big shopping brands, stand in line impatiently, and then rush out. Hardly do we notice the cashier. It's an anonymous face, and we most often don't see twice. We won't have a relationship with that person, nor would we try to establish one. People in line behind us are starting to get nervous, even upset if we engage in a conversation with the cashier longer than 10 seconds.

If we don't have a partner or a family, we come home feeling lonely. We turn on the TV, indulge us with Internet news stories, or check online dating websites. Transactions have replaced our relationship encounters during our daily lives. We pick the product, ask for the service, and hand over the money – done. With the instant click and order process online, we don't even see another face. We now have instant gratification but lost any form of sincere relationship.

Business these days is defined as making money. Who then needs people, besides the ones handing you over the money? Business was intended to be about service - service to others not to oneself!

People think it's cool to attend business meetings with an intention. For example: ,I am going to sell 100 of my new product.' With that, you are unconsciously setting yourself up to manipulate all other parties of this meeting. It's an insane transactional game that only serves the purpose of one person. You don't care about the others joining the meeting. It's a sick game that leads only to winners and losers with short-term results but lacks the foundation of working together. No significant purpose ever can be accomplished with this narcissistic behavior.

Text messaging and programs like WhatsApp are now used to send marriage proposals, even worse, to deliver the break up of a relationship. Conveniently, without seeing or facing your partner. The phone already left out the eye contact, but we can still notice the tone of the voice on the other end and may sense a feeling or emotion behind it. Text, even used with emojis leaves us stripped down to transactional value, and should be used only for that purpose. Without facing your fear and your partner's response, you soon lose the ability to have deep and meaningful conversations.

Does it matter if people, which are not part of your social circle, care about you? How would you feel about losing a job, and not one person is caring about it? We are ending up more lonely, deprived and depressed than ever, and need more stimuli and entertainment to cover up that gaping black hole in our hearts.

If you want people to care about you, care about the people! Start making time for conversations with people that you meet during your day. Make an effort to find out how they are doing. The convenient ‚I am doing great‘ phrase isn't cutting it. Mean it, try to connect with the person on an essential level - their heart. It feels real and nourishes the other person, and it makes you feel even better.

We have been taught what makes us happy comes from the outside world in the form of shopping, good grates and compliments – and so we shop for it. We have become feel-good shoppers.

What makes a lasting change about how you feel yourself is the act of being kind to other people, to be emphatic and generous. By activating these virtues, you are connecting with your own heart, and it instantly rewards you. It's one of the most critical metaphysical lessons you can learn:

Only what you are not giving can be lacking in any situation.

From Short-Term to Long-Term Thinking

„The poor plan for the weekend, the middle class plans for retirement and the wealthy plan for generations." - Author unknown

Short term goals can only lead to small changes, where long-term goals can lead to significant jumps and improvements. How much can you change when you focus on a weekly goal? How much can you accomplish when you focus on quarterly revenue statistics?

Our western lifestyle offers ample resources, products, and services. Gigantic shopping malls are filled with every product one can imagine. Most of the available products don't even fit into the shelves anymore. If there is scarcity, then it's in our mind.

Quantity Versus Quality

When you focus on short-term goals, you cannot think much about quality. How does quality bring in more money? More money comes in by selling more products. More money comes in by eliminating the secretary on the reception with an automated answering machine. More money comes in by adding pop-up boxes to web pages to gather email addresses.

These methods all lead to selling more products and adding more money for our companies. But is that true for the long term as well? Usually, it's a destructive spiral downwards that ends in a disaster. When a company eliminates the person on the reception with an automated phone system it will lose more customers over the long run. We all know the experience of outsourced phone support, and I don't know anybody who is not frustrated by it.

We immediately identify the inadequate support of the company. We immediately lower our value or appreciation for this company. When we continue to have more bad experiences, we start to hate the company. If we do not have a contract, we try to get out and switch to another company. We also start talking about our bad experience with friends and share it online. One negative comment on the Internet can harm a company today more than ever. It can spread like wildfire in seconds all over the globe. Many companies are realizing this already, and shifting their focus and attention back to better customer service.

Companies spend lot's of money to acquire customers. They are starting to make a profit only after a year or two - in some cases even longer. A customer that feels being held hostage is using the first chance to break free from the company. It's the feeling of freedom that makes us stick around.

We no longer have to focus on quantity. Quantity has become a no-brainer because robots and automated assembly lines are doing this for us. 3D printers will soon be able to create unlimited new products. The only reason we still focus on quantity is the out-dated monetary system, which is based on creating scarcity.

Indeed, we can, and have printed as much money as we want! That's not the issue. It's the system that regulates the money supply and the mathematical formula of interest that creates scarcity. If you have not yet fully understood the concept of money creation, please read the first few chapters again.

See The Bigger Picture

Focusing on the bigger picture helps you to see how the world and you are functioning. The more you expand your focus beyond yourself, the more you see. You will discover many new exciting things you can explore and pursue further. The world an all its possibilities are opening up to you. Shift your attention away from yourself, and you will forget your challenges and problems.

By focusing on a more significant challenge your power increases dramatically, and you will do things that seemed impossible to you before. An incredible amount of motivation arises, and you suddenly feel you have a purpose in life. We are not meant to live isolated and focused on ourselves. We forgot that life is not about getting a job, that it's about contributing to others and society. We forgot to question ourselves if what we are doing is helping or providing to a better world.

Don't wait until society changes for you. Don't wait until the economic situation improves, and don't wait for the next president to make a difference – most likely it won't happen.

Ask yourself: ‚Is your work contributing to a better world, to a higher standard of living and an expansion of abundance?' Take a good look at your workplace and honestly question yourself if this is your highest potential in action. If it's not, how do you justify doing it – besides exchanging your time for money?

What will happen if you don't focus on getting a paycheck or have security? What if you focus on the idea of contribution? Would that make a difference in your decision?

The Top to Bottom Model is Crumbling

An indicator of the current paradigm shift is the crumbling and imploding of the old top to bottom structure. Laws, rules and all significant changes came from the top. It was either a regime change, a new philosophy or a new economic model that was introduced from the top. The shift that's slowly happening now is the beginning of a bottom to the top phenomenon. Innovation, power, and change are starting to come from the people and will eventually dedicate who and what is on top.

In its final state - give it some time - it will be the total empowerment of every single person on the planet. Think about the vast information you can now access with a $100 smartphone in seconds. The processing power is likely 1000 times higher than all the NASA computers that were involved in the first manned moon landing.

This driving force is getting more powerful by the second with every single person changing their bottom line from making money to being of service to the greater good of all people. It will eventually transform our societies, our economics, and the way we think about leaders and governments. It will give birth to new regulations and leaders through our actions that are in alignment with our new bottom line.

If we refuse to accept the limitations of our current system, what do you think will happen? What if we start declining inhuman and immoral jobs that only lead to the destruction of our earth? These jobs and the companies that provided it will disappear! You can complain as much as you want, and as long as you want about the miserable economy. If you are accepting a job based on fear, you are contributing to creating more limitation. You are making limitation a reality. How would history have unfolded, if Rosa Parks had not refused to give up her seat for a white person?

Think about the following: The only thing that can be missing is what I am not giving.

Any shortage, lack or scarcity we experience is a result of our beliefs. The more we focus on the scarcity of things, the worse it will get. Wherever your attention goes, it grows. The more you focus on creating abundance, the more you will create. Building wealth is a natural flow of your creativity that can only be stopped by your concepts and beliefs.

How to Escape the Rat Race

Short-term thinking will keep you forever in the rat race. Even you manage to make it until the end of the months and pay all your bills – the next month it starts all over again. It never ends until you are in retirement – if you are lucky and have enough money left. Don't assume you are finally living your dreams once you are retired. Most likely it will be too late by then.

The moment you step out of the belief that your paycheck limits your income, you already planting a seed for expansion in your income. Don't worry how this will happen.

It's not even slightly crucial at that point. It's your expanding belief that will set up the conditions and create its reality.

Although the modern world has been created by the ingenuity of generations of hard-working people, few people nowadays have the patience to study, practice, and perfect skills. Young people want to achieve in just a decade the level of wealth it took their parents a lifetime to accomplish. This led to people making all sorts of economic short-cuts, including fraudulent practices in corporate boardrooms that affect stock exchanges, and with that, millions of other people.

Short term goals can only lead to small changes, where long-term goals can lead to significant jumps, vast improvements, and innovations. How much can you change when you focus on a weekly goal? How much can you accomplish when you only focus on quarterly revenue statistics? What changes in your thinking and plans if your goals exceed your lifespan?

Again, we don't have to focus on quantity any longer. Volume is now a no-brainer as robots, and automated assembly lines are doing this for us. We now have 3D printers that spit out an endless supply of new products 24/7. The only reason why we still focus on quantity is the monetary system, which is based on creating scarcity. Companies artificially lower the supply to sell it at a higher price. Many products, including food, gets dumped unused.

Focus on the quality of products and services, and your power increases dramatically. You will do things that seemed impossible before. You will have an incredible amount of motivation, and you will suddenly feel that you have a purpose in life. We human beings are not meant to live isolated and focused on ourselves. That's the big dreadful side effects of our society and the structures we build in the last 100 years. We forgot that life is not about getting a job, that it's about contributing to the overall good of society. We forgot to question if what we are doing is contributing.

Contributing to a better world leads to abundance, focusing on the old instinct of fear of survival leads to scarcity.

Limitations Exists Only in Your Mind

What happens if you do not focus on getting a paycheck or have security? What if you focus on the idea of contribution? Would that create a different experience in your life?

The old economic structure of top to bottom is crumbling. The laws, the rules and the changes always came from the top. It was either a regime change, a new philosophy or a new economic model. The shift we are seeing happening now is the start of a bottom to the top phenomenon.

Again, think about the incredible information power you have available now, even with the cheapest smartphone. You can access almost all information that exists within seconds. This wasn't available 20 years ago. You had to go to a library, and it contained a very limited assortment of books compared to what information is available worldwide now.

We are in the process of changing the bottom line. More and more organizations and people worldwide are seeing the long-term trap of making money the bottom line. They all have made contributions and love their bottom line. The best example is the open source movement, where people contribute their intelligence to serve the better good of all.

The Open Source Movement

Open source is a proven alternative to commercial software in a variety of sectors, and it's growing fast. In fact, a recent survey found that almost 70% of corporate organizations are either contributing to or participating in open-source projects.

The beauty of open source resides in the fact that its code is open, mostly free and can always be tweaked, modified, optimized, and customized to your needs. Over the years, open-source communities and supporters have grown significantly regarding size, responsiveness, and expertise. These enthusiastic and passionate experts ensure that the product you use consistently meets the highest-quality standards, even as new technologies emerge, which threaten to make old tools obsolete.[63]

The ability to customize an open-source project is one of its most significant benefits. This aspect of the open software is not limited to initial development, but instead is something that can be done continuously over time, as new forms of media and communication channels emerge, and your organization develops new needs. There is also the added benefit of expanding the platform around your vision, not that of a commercial vendor, and also being able to create your timelines for innovation.

Open Source Ecology

An open source economy is an efficient economy which increases innovation by open collaboration. To get there, OSE is currently developing a set of open-source blueprints for the Global Village Construction Set (GVCS) – a collection of the 50 most important machines that it takes for modern life to exist – everything from a tractor to an oven, to a circuit maker.[64]

There are many great examples that I would love to add here, but it would go beyond the scope of this book. Just look at what the WordPress community created.

The lack on the outside is a direct result of the lack inside of ourselves. The more we focus on the lack of things, the worse it gets. The more you focus on creating abundance, the more of it you will create. Building wealth is a natural flow of your creativity, and can only be stopped by your limiting concepts and beliefs.

Short-term thinking will also keep you in the rat race as long as you live. Once you managed to make it until the end of the months and pay all of your bills, the next month it starts all over again. It never ends until you are too old to work, and that's what you call retirement. Don't assume you are going to live your dreams once you are retired.

Don't you feel that there is more in life than where you are right now? And that's a good thing to acknowledge. Honesty to yourself and others always gets you exactly what you need to flourish in life. Sometimes you may not see this when it happens, but after a few months or even years have passed, you look back and see that it was a beautiful thing that happened to you. Speaking the truth is challenging, but it leads to the right outcome, even you may not see or understand it.

The moment you step out of the belief that your income is limited by your paycheck you are already planting a seed for your liberation. It's the expanding belief that will set up the conditions to create it in your life.

Long-term success for all is only possible when you reintroduce creative thinking, feeling, and behavior into this world. Instant gratification is a trap that avoids building real wealth.

It's not about how fast you can get from A to B. It's about how much enjoyment you and others can have and share on the path from A to B. On the fast road other people are obstacles in your way, on the slow road other people become your friends.

When you are going to make little decisions wait at least 1-2 minutes. If you make more substantial decisions give it at least a day rest. If you make significant life-changing choices let it be idle for at least one to two weeks.

From Consuming to Creating Value

„If we can fall in love with serving people, creating value, solving problems, building valuable connections and doing work that matters, it makes it far more likely we're going to do important work." - Seth Godin, American author

Taking versus Giving

Taking is the fastest way to get something, right? From a short-term perspective that may be true, in the long run, it's not. It directly leads to limited resources and scarcity. If we only take, who then creates or supplies what we take? One of the worst concepts of society is naming people consumer.

The Lake Example

Let's compare humanity and all available resources with a lake. For simplicity let's assume 100 people represent all of humanity. A pond with 100 fishes serves the planet's entire resources.

Let's further assume that every single person is taking a worm on their fishing rod and tries to catch a fish. If we had an evenly distributed experience, every person could have caught one fish and would be happy for one today.

Already by the next day everybody would be miserable and starve because there a no more fish left to catch. Everyone is only thinking for them self, and there is nothing left for anybody the next day. It's a very short win situation followed by a massive loss situation.

's either only short-term thinking or a complete lack of understanding that makes us behave in such a stupid way.

Now consider the example of focusing on giving instead of taking. In our lake example, you could be part of creating a fish farm. You could invest or be part of the working force. Establishing a fish farm would be one idea of creating an endless supply of fishes.

Now you, and all the other 99 people could fish and have a meal today, and every day after that. It's a win-win situation. Everyone including yourself will have a better living situation. It will create abundance by making sure there is forever ample supply.

Nature Is Abundance

Nature shows us precisely that. Millions of seeds fall from only one tree, land on the fertile ground, and create plenty of new trees. There will always be an ample supply of trees. There are no regulations necessary to make this happen. It's just following nature's principle of abundance.

The old paradigm of 'taking' does no longer work. It leads to a state of being poor, keeps you poor, selfish and fearful. It arrives from the belief that you are isolated and separated from the rest of the world and must always act on your own. Taking is an unconscious survival mode, which leads to scarcity and results in being unhappy, dissatisfied and unfulfilled. The mentality of 'taking' also comes from an unconscious belief that you don't have the power to create. It's the mindset of being a consumer and not a producer.

With the beginning of the industrialization process, we have entered a new state of the economy, which is quickly optimizing itself to produce more products and services in less time. It also means less human intervention. All jobs that can be replaced by robots and artificial intelligence powered machines will soon be gone.

Entering Stage Three of Human Evolution

We are in one of the most significant evolutionary processes the world has ever seen. Over the next 20 years, you will see radical changes on this planet. All old structures will fade out, fail or simply become obsolete. Many industries will be completely wiped out. Peter Diamondis [65] believes that 40% of all fortune 500 companies will be gone in the next decade.

The next evolutionary stage, which is already starting to take effect, are efficiency, optimization, and global connectivity. What's interesting is that the more we all grow together as one humanity, the more we all become empowered. We each find our individuality in the process of being of service to the global network. I call this the third stage of human evolution.

The first stage was the collective state, where the Gods influenced our thinking and acting. We lived as a collective in groups, and the influence of the environment determined our life. We slept when it was getting dark, and we ate when we hunted or gathered food.

The second sate was the individualization process. It was the beginning of living independent from nature, and over time lead to the method of controlling nature. We lifted ourselves up from the influence of the environment and started to shape it to our needs, wishes, and ideas.

As we come to see now, without nature, we are missing a big piece of life itself. We also recognize that controlling nature backfires more often than we can handle. We come to understand that we can't disconnect from nature and the collective forces that thrive through it. We now realize that nature itself is a thriving force in the universe and we human beings are an essential part of it.

Therefore, stage three of the evolution of the human species is the combination of the collective and the individual. It is the realization that we are all unique and each of us has its gifts, talents, and abilities. This new concept means that each of us is contributng to the collective. Life now means for each of us to add to a new state of intelligence, which allows natural abundance again to flow and evolve.

Looking for a job is an outdated concept, and it will be harder and harder to accomplish, as we eliminate anything that stands between the person that looks for a product or service, and the person or company that provides it.

Focus on Efficiency

Nature shows us that economy means efficiency. It doesn't waste anything and optimizes itself to create with minimum effort. It finds the best possible way to achieve its goal. The way our economy works is highly inefficient because way too many resources are wasted, and way too much regulations are in place.

Tesla is revolutionizing the car industry. Not only is Tesla the first new car company in the United States that went public since Ford in 1956, Tesla also left the old concept of combustion engine behind, and concentrated its effort on building the best electric cars on the planet. Tesla is eliminating the need for dealerships, oil changes, and inspections.

They are also the first car company to deliver car updates over the air. It eliminates the costly and burdensome effort to get your car to the dealership in case of a safety recall. The current car business model was built around oil, creating jobs around it, and has not changed since its invention almost 130 [66] years ago.

Did you know, that electricity powered the first cars? At that time they only had one significant disadvantage. The distance you could travel was insufficient because of the limited capacity of the batteries, and soon gasoline powered vehicles provided much longer travel distance. The car industry convinced the government that cars offer a much better experience to the individual than public transportation. Soon, the government started to build roads for the vehicles. It was a very aggressive move toward cars. An example of this bold move was the building of bridges over streets in places that lead to suburban areas, which were constructed low in height. The purpose? Public buses could not pass through!

Before the United States expanded its car industry, there was public transportation and it was working excellent. Now, that the individual transportation idea has hit the wall, what's next is public transits again. Elon Musk, the founder of Tesla knows this and has already started a new company, and this could be the next evolutionary step in transportation - it's called Hyperloop.

A Hyperloop[67] is a proposed mode of passenger and freight transportation, comprised in a sealed tube or system of tubes through which a pod may travel free of air resistance or friction, conveying people or objects at high speed while being very efficient.

Think about all the precious resources that are wasted to build cars, which just last about ten years. An average of 1.6 person[68] drives it, and most of the time it sits somewhere idle where you could have green landscape. Also, think about how rapidly they fall apart, not to mention the many useless oil changes. The car industry can build an engine that runs with 100% synthetic oil, and it can last a lifetime. Why then do we still need oil changes? Because the car industry works hand in hand with the oil industry.

Start Contributing

The principle of contribution works all the time, and for your entire life. It keeps you evolving and allows collaboration with others. There is no need to focus on fairness, as it takes out the divide between you and the other person. You are working from the same perspective, and you are aligned in your purpose with others.

Most people say: „I want to contribute, but I first need to make money for it." Again, that's backward thinking, and will never get you there. They never get the money because they are always focused on themselves.

There is an Indian proverb that illustrates this. If you see a problem, and you don't do anything about it, you become part of the problem.

Whenever I see people and friends going through times of depression, it's always the issue of the mind being entirely focused on their problems. These depressions dissolve in a matter of days, or even hours, by shifting the perspective away from themselves. Issues and challenges are never solved on the same level where they occur. You have to expand and shift your attention away from yourself. Depression can be a sign of being stuck with yourself.

Creating value is a surefire way to creating wealth.

Start Creating Value

Creating is an advanced stage after you have tried balancing giving and taking. You either bring something new into existence, or you improve on something that already existed.

The most important skill you can develop is to create value for other people. Get into the mindset of other people. Understand their viewpoint on life or their perspective of the situation or problem that they are trying to overcome or solve. Think about what you can create, produce, process, or offer as a service that helps people to eliminate fear, discomfort, and isolation. Give them joy, comfort, peace, etc. In our hearts, we all want the same.

When you create value, you are building an asset. An asset is something that holds value. Assets that are of high importance to society usually through off money or benefit in any form, e.g., dividends, royalties, etc. Assets are a support system for yourself and others. Think about the lake example I illustrated before.

Assets have real, sustainable true value! Money is not an asset - it's not wealth!

Innovate things! We are currently experiencing one of the most significant shifts on a global scale, where we move away from physical skills toward intellectual skills. Most physical work is already on its way to being outsourced to millions of robots and artificially intelligent machines.

Knowledge is a form of currency and an asset of the future. It takes at least 4-5 years to become an expert in an area of life. Teach information, coaching and mentoring.

In your work choose long-term trends of 10-20 years, maybe even 50 or 100 years. Most schools teach you things that are obsolete by the time you are finished studying. The Internet is still in its infant state with its current technology and usage. Make it better – innovate it, simplify it or improve it.

Question to find your gifts and talents:

- What are you good at?
- What would you love to do even you would not get paid?
- What would you do if you had an unlimited amount of money?
- What would you do if you had only six months to live?
- What did you like the most when you were a kid?

Try to understand people's problems:

- Ask them: ‚What is your biggest fear or frustration?'
- Ask them: ‚What would be the ideal outcome?'

Your most important asset is your inner value, experience, and knowledge. The moment you focus on cultivating and contributing your assets, you will start the process of creating outer assets. Master these areas in your life - one step at a time. Pick a topic and learn it until you become good at it. Break it down from large chunks into small steps so you can manage it.

At the risk of repeating myself, creating value for others is the most rewarding task you can ever do. Not only is it satisfying, but it also serves as a source for your prosperity. If you make new decisions in your life that lead to creating value for others, be prepared for significant changes to happen. Very often first things have to get worse, or fall apart, before there is room to create something better.

Deliberately abandon destructive and opposing habits. Get rid of unnecessary stuff, move them out of your way. If you don't do this consciously, very often they will be removed for you by other people or circumstances and cause you suffering.

Nothing belongs to you; you are only the Stuart of it.

Take risks! Don't play safe! Manage risk, don't avoid it. Your own experience is the most important. The physical reality is only here to make this experience possible. If you face an obstacle, learn a new skill that will overcome that obstacle. Your greatest asset is yourself!

To sum it up...

- Wealth comes not from getting money; it comes from creating value
- Keeping your wealth in money reduces its value
- If you use money you lose money (fees)
- Turn money into assets
- Overcome your negative emotions
- Go deep with your creative outlook
- Pick a long-term trend
- Invest in learning - at least five years on a topic that interests you
- Persist - learn from any failure and stay on the path to wealth
- Get around experts that know what you want to do
- Keep experiencing the edge of your comfort zone
- Don't let yourself stop by fear - step into it
- Create value every day in every area of your field of expertise

Wealth Creation Business Plan

Create a long-term plan for how you will create value and wealth for yourself and others. This will be one of the most critical steps in your path to becoming wealthy. Keep in mind, the value of planning does not come from the plan itself. It comes from the process of making the plan; it's what you learn from it.

Take a notebook out right now and answer these questions:

- What are my inherent gifts and talents?
- What am I really good at?
- How I can serve others?
- What have I given up?
- What can I do to eliminate pain, suffering, and unhappiness in the world?
- Do I have relationships with wealthy people?
- What skills do I need to develop next?
- How do I develop these skills?
- What's my long-term wealth (business) plan?
- What would need to happen in my life to make this all inevitable?

Chapter IV - The Laws of Metaphysics

Blank Paper Versus Acorn Analogy

"It is not until you change your identity to match your life blueprint that you will understand why everything in the past never worked."
- Shannon L. Alder, Inspirational author

The „Blank Paper" Metaphor

The basic concept or belief system that has been taught to us from childhood on is the idea that we come into this world like a fresh, clean and empty sheet of paper. We are nothing - blank - like anybody else. The only element that sets us apart from each other is, apparently how we look. Some even go as far as to acknowledge that we have different talents and interests, but that's already the end of the line.

We usually start filling this blank sheet of paper with rules and guidelines from any authorities we can find in our society. The do's and don'ts, the should and shouldn't, and of course the physical laws of nature. Furthermore, on top of all these 'borrowed' concepts, we have to define who we are. We have to develop a personality and an identity. We have to establish an idea of how we create ourselves.

Kids often get asked: „What would you like to become when you grow up and be an adult?" Here are some typical examples of parental guidelines:

- Get a good education so you can get a decent job
- Study even longer, and you can be a lawyer or a doctor
- Don't do anything stupid, do what has been proven before
- Don't even think about being an artist
- Make as much money as possible; it buys almost everything
- Stay away from drugs it gets you killed or in prison

- Make sure you save enough money for retirement
- Be nice to others, so they like you
- Try harder than the others
- Get married and have children

In your early childhood, you may still enjoy some freedom, because you are not yet bothered by these questions. Already in kindergarten teacher are trying hard to get your mind set up for analytical processing, and to be prepared for the adult battlefield.

Your heart or soul is not required for this system to work. This whole concept turns you into a soulless being. It creates human beings that function more or less like machines. You have no real sense of who you are. You become exchangeable with anybody else that was able to retrofit their blank paper with the same programming.

With this conditioning – in the not so far future – an artificially intelligent machine or robot will most likely replace you. It can do your work longer, better and faster. Besides that, machines and robots don't complain, need no lunch breaks, and don't ask for an increase in salary.

It's a path that leads to a senseless, heartless, and meaningless society that has no real purpose and vision of life. It leads to a community that is driven by fear, scarcity, and limitation. In other words, a society that we have right now.

This paper analogy goes back to the age of Newton - the mechanical worldview. It's the result of a core belief that has shaped our current world paradigm. To bring this mechanical worldview into existence, scientists and philosophers of this age had to leave out the heart and the soul of the equation.

Our current worldview is an insufficient idea, and we are already shifting away from it. Over time this worldview usually expands, however, it seems that sometimes we ‚forget' aspects we already learned.

We are facing incredible problems as a society, tremendous challenges for the earth and devastating personal struggle caused by our concept of life.

Life Perspective from the „Paper Viewpoint"

- You have to become someone
- You have to strive to be better than others
- You have to compete with others
- You can't trust anybody
- You are fighting against your nature
- You see and face life as a constant battle
- You have to prove to others that you are special
- You need to be in constant control

The „Acorn Metaphor"

What is much closer to the truth of nature, and who we are, is the model of the acorn. An acorn holds inside itself the blueprint to become an oak tree. It cannot become anything else than an oak tree. It does not question what it should become. It has inbuilt intelligence that holds the information on how to become a perfect oak tree. Do you think a baby is busy with figuring out how to become a child or an adult? It happens naturally, on its own.

Every seed and cell on the planet holds this kind of information. It is the marvelous wonder of nature, and the organized universe behind it, that makes this possible. Do you think we human beings are an exception to this? As mentioned before, there is a reason that every human looks unique. It's an expression of its inherent uniqueness. Don't you think that's true for what's inside ourselves as well?

Every seed, every tree, every flower, every snowflake, and every human is unique. Because everything in nature – including us – is special, nothing is special at all. It means you do not have to do anything to become special – you are already unique.

Every attempt to become something special is denying who you are. Every effort to become something else than who you already are is a colossal struggle. You are wasting your precious time and resources. It is a self-chosen path against nature, and against your destiny. You are trying to serve two masters - the human belief system of fear and lack and the divine reality of love and abundance. Living according to the false notion that we have to go outside ourselves to get what we want has led to the experience of lack, limitations, greed, and conflict.

In the western world, we have more abundance than at any time in history, yet we are some of the unhappiest people on the planet. Millions of people only survive with anti-depressive medicine.

We have evolved to a place where we must co-create with the evolutionary impulse to fulfill our destiny. We must give up the belief that the world is happening to us, and realize that we are happening in the world.

When you tap into your true vision, the possibilities are endless, because true vision is not something you make up, it's something you're made of. It's the true nature and essence, the seat of your soul, and the source of your power.

The universe is not neutral. It has a plan, a pattern, an evolutionary idea, seeking willing places for its ever-expanding expression. There is some invisible force that is moving every aspect of reality to its next best expression. When you stay the course, no matter what, you reach your destination. It's about creating a life structure that mirrors our soul's blueprint.

Life doesn't hold anything back from us, we hold ourselves back from life.

Life Perspective from the „Acorn Viewpoint"

- You are already special
- You have unique gifts and talents
- The purpose of your life is to express your gifts and talents
- Your nature is to be in collaboration with others
- Life is a given, and you can relax into it

Who You Think You Are Defines Your Life Experience

„What a liberation to realize that the 'voice in my head' is not who I am. 'Who am I, then?' The one who sees that." - Eckhart Tolle, Spiritual teacher

Have you ever thought about who you are? I mean beyond your personality and your identity? Do you think the brain, that holds your mind is the center of who you are? If you replace one or more of your organs with that from a donor – would you agree with me that – you are still the same person? How about an arm or a leg? Yes, still the same person?

Soon, we may be able to replace any body part - besides the brain. Let's assume that we have replaced all your body parts and the only 'original' part that's left is your brain. That would leave us with the only option to look for who you are in the brain.

Let's expand this idea to feelings and emotions. At this point, we have to assume that they also originate from the brain, because it's the only part we have not replaced yet. Can you be aware of your feelings? Of course, you can! You can observe them, which means that feelings are not you, otherwise who is observing?

Let's move on to thoughts. Can you be aware of your thoughts? Close your eyes for a moment and tell your mind 'I am thinking right now.' You are still there - somewhere - observing telling yourself 'I am thinking.' Now that leaves us with the notion that you also not your thoughts!

It leaves us now with the question what is there left that can be you? Maybe your memories, all of your experiences since you are born? If that would be the case, then you would be not you when you were born. Which would further indicate that a baby would have no individuality? Have you ever looked at a babies face? Would you argue with me that there is ,someone' there besides a body?

Let's recap where we are in our investigation. You are neither your body, nor your feelings and thoughts, nor your memories and experiences.

Do you agree with me that there is a ,presence' already right after birth? Does this 'presence' appear at birth or is it already present in the womb? If you are a mother, you know the answer already, because you have experienced your baby being in the womb. Does this ,presence' arrive at the ninth month? Sixth months? First month?

One more step down the rabbit hole and we come to the point of conception. This is where the semen and the egg come together. Two cells come together, and the ,you' gets established, somehow? A slippery road that leaves the big question: „Where are you?"

Your Genetic Blueprint

Bruce Lipton's ground-breaking scientific experiments prove our genes are not the brain of our cells as our biology books continue to teach us. Experimenting with cells, he took out the nucleus, only to discover that the cells continue to live for weeks.

His conclusion is obvious – the nucleus with its DNA is not the brain of the cell and therefore does not control the cell.

Biology is finally turning into a paradigm shift, giving up the theory that we are all controlled by our genes. If our genes determine happiness, then at the moment we are born, our happiness unfolds according to the program of the genes. There is nothing we can do about it. It already sets the state of victimhood in life.

The nucleus of the cell contains 50% DNA and 50% protein. Scientists have analyzed the cell, and in doing so, looked only at the DNA - discarding the proteins. The DNA is the reproductive system for the proteins. If a protein is not available but is needed for environmental response, it can be built from the blueprint that the DNA provides.

So, what is controlling the cell? Astonishing as it sounds, it is the environment and its perception of it! The perception of the cell is experienced through the skin. The skin contains hundreds of proteins that act as preceptors and effectors. Environmental signals like temperature and light trigger preceptors. These original signals are then translated into the cell becoming a secondary signal, activating the protein to do something, for example, to break apart an enzyme. [69]

Your Perception is Influenced by Your Beliefs

We are all made up of trillions of cells. Our bodies and organs share the same pattern. There is one big difference, and that is our ability to perceive an environmental signal. Our beliefs influence perception. I can experience a healthy environment and at the same time believe it is not healthy for me.

By believing this, I am changing my perception, and therefore changing my cellular behavior. A specific protein for example that is necessary to build my immune system cannot be reproduced. That leads to a reduced immune system and might be the beginning of a dis-ease.

Cells have two basic behaviors: growth and protection. The cell can only choose one at a time, either it is in growth mode or protection mode. There are other behaviors, more neutral, but not relevant for understanding our current scenario.

Our system cannot grow if we are in protection mode!

Protection mode is another form of stress - like fear. If our system is in constant stress mode, then there is no possibility to grow. However growth is an essential part of our evolutionary survival strategy, and if we are not growing, we are stagnating and setting the stage for a dis-ease in the future.

It is a faulty assumption that our genes control us. There are no cancer genes. It is not possible for a gene to activate or change on its own, for example, producing cancer. It is the environmental signal and our perception (belief) that contributes to a change in our system.[70]

Perception is highly influenced by our beliefs, therefore beliefs control your genes!

The bottom line is this; we are all powerful. We have power over the unfoldment of our life. We have control over which genes can be activated. We are not the victims of our genes. What we have to do is select the appropriate beliefs according to our environment and our unique, inherent blueprint.

Your Energetic Blueprint

A blueprint refers to the genetic and energetic composition of who you are. From the physical viewpoint, it's common sense that you have a unique set of DNA. It contains the genetic structure, which determines your physical structure. But the DNA also holds a genetic structure, which we can't measure yet. It's a particular energy field that correlates with the DNA. The DNA may be only the physical representation of this energetic field.

It's like a hologram; you can't see it until light illuminates it. The light resonant with the field and makes it appear for our eyes in a three-dimensional form. The information within a hologram is not stored at a specific place; it's everywhere. That's why you can use only parts of a hologram, and it will still generate the complete picture.

You can compare it with the blueprint from a house, or any industrial design application. It's a design pattern, which holds the key elements to build and replicate it into physical form. When you create a house, you start with an idea. How should the rooms be laid out, should it be energy efficient. Maybe you want rounded corners and french doors. With that idea in mind, you look for an architect, who will draw up a blueprint.

This plan has to be very precise. It needs to contain the orientation, the measurements, the floor plan, the electric wiring, the plumbing and so on.

If you know your intrinsic blueprint, which holds your unique talents, gifts, and abilities, you have the foundation for what you can build and create in your life.

What happens when you use the blueprints from other people? They interfere with your blueprint. It causes confusion, irritation and the feeling of being lost. It's a conflict between your most inner guidance system - something you can sense - and the intellectual ideas and concepts from others. You are in conflict with your intrinsic blueprint. It causes friction, frustration, and failure.

Being in touch with your intrinsic blueprint is experienced as a natural desire. What follows is pure happiness and lasting fulfillment, which does not originate from the outside world. You are therefore programmed for success if you stay within your path. Your talents, gifts, and abilities are part of the inherent genes and its energetic blueprint. It's therefore no longer the question of who you want to become - you know who you are, and your purpose is to express this in life.

Conscious Versus Subconscious

Your thoughts have the power to manifest your reality, and most of your thoughts originate from your subconscious mind. Studies confirm that you are using your conscious mind only to 5%, and your conscious mind is where your desires and aspirations reside.

The conscious mind is the latest evolution of the brain and represents you as an individual, a unique entity. The conscious mind is also the creative mind. It contains your wishes, desires, and aspirations for life. The conscious mind is very slow and has only a limited capacity to learn new things. The conscious mind is good for one thing only, and that is thinking and paying attention.

The subconscious mind is profoundly connected with habits. When you repeat things over and over again – it will lead to the development of a pattern. A pattern or habit is a program in the subconscious mind. When you receive a stimulus, and there is a habit in the subconscious mind related to that stimulus, it will automatically engage you in that habit.

You can change your conscious mind with ease. It's much harder to make changes in your subconscious mind. There is a simple reason for that. Just imagine if you learn to walk, and the next day you would have to start learning it again – very inefficient of course. That's why habits stored in the subconscious mind are not easy to change. Once a program like walking has been established, it will work automatically and be fully functioning - day after day.

The subconscious mind is also million times faster than the conscious mind. Imagine a tennis player and the reaction time to hit the ball that comes with 150 mph – it's just a few milliseconds. It would be impossible to hit the ball by thinking about its speed, the curve and where it may impact the racket.

The subconscious mind holds all your individual experiences. It's a personal storage of all your habits, beliefs and concepts that you are not aware.

When you create anything in your life, the success is determined by the following three factors.

1. Your thoughts - coming from your conscious mind
2. Your beliefs, habits and concepts - coming from your subconscious mind
3. Collective beliefs and concepts - coming from the collective unconscious mind

Creating abundance in your life is a natural process of allowing changes in your life to happen without resistance. As we are creatures of habit, our habits from the past may not align with the changes in life.

Change, wise people say, is the only constant in life. We all in our western society have a huge problem with change. We don't embrace it. After we have suffered years of dull-

ress education from school, continued to work at the job we don't like, we finally want to see the results of our effort. Sadly, in the lives of most people, that never happens.

To step out of this devastating cycle - some gave it the name rat race - you are required to replace destructive and unsupportive patterns with helpful and supportive ones. It's not something that can be done by just reading a book. It's constant training of your mind until your brain has developed new neural pathways, which then lead to automatic behavior that are in alignment with life and your purpose in life. Many go to the gym to keep their body in shape, but they hardly pay attention to the fitness level of their mind!

Use Your Inherent Guidance System

Use your conscious mind to make choices that are in alignment with your internal guidance system, which is your heart and gut feeling. The simplest way to accomplish this is by slowing down, which increases your awareness. Success in life is determined by making conscious choices.

Don't worry about figuring out how, and don't worry how it will come into existence. Life itself is intelligent and far more capable of creating the right circumstances than the few ideas you have in mind.

The World's Core Concepts - Separation Versus Oneness

„If you want to find the secrets of the universe, think in terms of energy, frequency and vibration." – Nikola Tesla, Serbian-American inventor, electrical engineer, mechanical engineer, physicist, and futurist

When you understand the difference between ‚separation' and ‚oneness,' you have the foundation to make your life a breeze. It's a very advanced metaphysical topic, and it may spin your head a bit. Let's start out with some basic definitions.

Oneness is the state that includes everything, is connected to everything, and is the source of everything. Many names from various cultures and times have been given to this state. It's the basic premise that everything in the universe is connected, even it seems separate to us. Quantum physics had proven this already 50 years ago!

Separation is the state where everything exists isolated and independent from each other. It's also called the dualistic concept, which means anything that I pick has at least two different aspects to it. For example, top and bottom, left and right, light and dark, good and evil, heaven and earth. The dualistic worldview is our primary education model.

The model of separation and the dualistic viewpoint it entails creates our fundamental belief system. Based on this belief system, we perceive our world and the whole cosmos we live. From the concept that we are separate from nature arrives the arrogant attitude, that we can do better. We control, harvest and monetize nature. That's why it's ‚normal' for us to burn down the forest, pollute air and water, and destroy entire habiats for animals. The belief we are separate from anything else leaves us with the notion hat we can do whatever we want, and it won't affect us.

That's not true, as we can now experience with almost 8.0 billion people on the planet. How could we? We all drink the same water, breath the same air, and use the same soil. It now just becomes more evident through the globalization effect. Today, we know any environmental disaster in the world in a few minutes, if not seconds. New products are launching now in 40-50 countries simultaneously.

Oneness From a Religious Perspective

Throughout the ages scriptures of all religions have proclaimed that humanity is one great family. The Dalai Lama expresses this beautifully. „All the world's major religions have a similar aim, so harmony between them is both important and necessary. I firmly believe, that although they may have substantial differences of philosophical outlook, all religions have the same potential to be of help to humankind. Each emphasizes methods for improving human beings by developing such qualities as generosity, love, compassion, and respect for others."

All beings want happiness and try to avoid suffering. This collective experience is reflected in the universal themes of love and compassion, found in all religions.

Live by the Golden Rule

The Golden Rule is the cornerstone of religious and metaphysical understanding. It is the complete expression of the ‚Oneness' of all people, serving as the foundation for peace and universal goodwill on earth. The Golden Rule is expressed almost word for word in every religion. It is fundamental to all religions.

„One should treat others as one would like others to treat oneself."

Jesus referred to The Golden Rule as "the law and the prophets." Mohammed described it as "the noblest expression of religion." Rabbi Hillel stated in the Jewish Talmud that

The Golden Rule is "the whole of the Torah and the remainder is but commentary." Vyasa, the enlightened Hindu sage, called it "the sum of all true righteousness." Similarly, Buddha referred to it as "the total sum of all righteousness." And Confucius, the great Chinese master, deemed it "the one principle upon which one's whole life may proceed." [71]

Many people are taught from childhood on that living 'The Golden Rule' is ideal, but the practical benefits are not emphasized enough - if at all. When people look upon others as extensions of themselves, all obstacles to fulfillment are removed - for individuals as well as for society. When the activities of every other person support the goal of every individual, the world can flourish with peace and prosperity. For this reason, The Golden Rule should not be thought of as a vague ideal. It is one of the most powerful principles, which embodies the most profound aspirations of humanity. It serves as the basis for all that is positive and lasting in human life. [72]

It's important that this rule is not only understood on a philosophical level, it has to be also understood from a scientific viewpoint. It has to be experienced to become part of us. It has to be recognized internally as the truth.

The Quantum Aspect of Oneness

Einstein concluded that space and time are intertwined, and that matter is inseparable from the quantum energy field. This is the sole reality underlying all appearances. Physicists found that the most basic atomic particles in the cosmos comprise the very fabric of the material universe. An electron, for example, can be shown to be both a wave and a particle depending on the observer's perspective.

What we perceive to be solid objects are in fact at the atomic level, not so solid at all. Atoms are 99.999999999999% empty space!

A mind-numbing idea, if you think about punching a brick wall. Even the simple act of sitting on a chair repels the idea that this is could all be empty space. What you are feel-ng is merely pressure. Forces interacting at an atomic level and your nerve endings are just reacting. Atoms are surrounded by shells of electrons that cause them to push away from one another. [73]

Since all matter and events interact with each other, time (past, present, and future) along with space and distance, all is relative to the observer and operate as one under the law of Non-Locality. The discovery of non-locality and the wave/particle duality means that everything is joined or connected.

Space and time are composed of the same essence as matter. The matter then is just an expression of dense essence.

Everything is connected to everything else, and physical reality is both - waves and particles. This model birthed the idea of the "holographic universe." The whole can invariably be found in the tiniest particles: an atom of a blade of grass to the most distant galaxies. The building blocks of atoms are mere, "parcels of compressed energy, packed and patterned according to certain mathematical formula." [74]

Matter and energy are two poles of the same unity. Shamans and mystics call this Oneness or Interconnectedness. It's also referred to as consciousness. Your sense of self and the continuity of experience is not contained within anything in your brain or body in any physical way, the cells of your body die and all the material that makes the tangible you is replaced continuously throughout your life.

It is consciousness that remains and gives you this experience.

What we experience as separate is an illusion. Since there is only a fundamental unity, then the idea that you are somehow different from the outside environment begins to fade. The earth in which you live is you, and you are the earth and everything within it. You are the universe, everything it takes to make a world is contained within all of us. Consciousness then has no boundaries. The only limit is your imagination.

Unravelling More Illusions

If we talk about God, which stands for unity, then again by its definition it enclose
everything else. It follows that there is no 'Eval' on the opposite side. It does not exist
and it is only a trap of our dualistic thinking. If we observe something as eval, it can jus
be the absence of God, and what causes it can only be the thoughts of our narrow, spli
mind.

We are used to focussing our minds on the details, and we don't see how profound ou
life is influenced and dictated by some of our core beliefs and viewpoints.

As long as you believe the 'outside' world is the cause that effects you, as long you experienc
being powerless. The truth is so frightening to us that we are always proving to yourself ane
others what we believe.

When you recognize this fundamental truth of oneness, your life becomes the expres
sion of it, and you are liberated from the illusion of boundaries. Boundaries then be
come a simple act of creating the experience you choose. They are no longer stumbling
stones in your way.

Going Beyond Illusions - From Fear to Love

"Our deepest fear is not that we are inadequate. Our deepest fear is that we are powerful beyond measure. It is our light not our darkness that most frightens us." - Marianne Williamson, American spiritual teacher, author, and lecturer

Motivation in life comes from two perspectives. It's either based on fear, which asks the primary question "How do I GET the most?" This type of motivation leads to scarcity and deficiency. Then there is the motivation based on love, with its primal questions: "How do I GIVE the most?" The source of this motivation leads to affluence and wealth.

These are the only two basic options, from where all our motivations derive. It is either fear or it is love. There is nothing else.

Every negative emotion is a derivative of fear, and every positive emotion is a derivative of love. In your body, you can feel the differences as contraction versus expansion. The motivation from fear correlates with the initial feeling of contraction. The motivation from love matches the feeling of expansion. All other feelings either originate from fear or love.

The book ‚A Course in Miracles' refers to love as the only thing that exists. Something that contains everything can have no opposite. Fear then does not exist, it is merely an illusion that derives from our mind. Love is connected to the heart and is based on oneness, fear is related to the mind and is based on duality. Fear can only come from the mind because it operates in the realm of duality.

Have you heard the saying: „The mind divides, and the heart unites"?

Love encompasses everything, and what encompasses everything can have no opposite. Which means, when your thinking arises from fear you are actually not thinking, you are hallucinating!

Fear can only exist in the absence of love. Love is always in its natural and original state where things just the way they are - free from any label or judgment.

Love is the state of being where you are one with everything else. It is therefore only possible to recognize when you fall out of that state. Fear is like a mental filter, a colored lens you look through. The word 'love' has been misinterpreted and misused over an extended period. It is now associated with hundreds of beliefs, concepts, and ideas. For example what someone does for someone else.

Ask a few people what love is, and you will see the wide selection of answers you get. The answers are most likely based on concepts, which have been indoctrinated from early childhood and school. They are usually based on external circumstances - on specific behaviors and actions.

The word 'love' and the root of it derive from ‚unity' and ‚oneness.' Other words describe the same. For example God, the universe, singularity, almighty, Lord, maker, divinity, holy spirit, universal life force, creator, supreme being, Allah, Jehovah and many more.

Light and Darkness

Love and fear can also be compared to light and darkness. Only light exists, darkness is not the opposite, it is the absence of light. When you have a dark room, and you turn on the light the darkness disappears. It only works in that direction. If you have a room with light, you can't bring darkness into it!

If this particular topic interests you, please feel free to take a closer look at the book 'A Course in Miracles.' As an entry point into this topic, I recommend you pick up a book from Marianne Williamson.

When you experience fear, then you have unconsciously chosen darkness. At this moment you identify yourself with a concept or belief, made up by your mind. Your mind gives you a reason, a belief or an idea of how you interpret a particular situation in your life.

It is a 'worldly' illusion, but it seems real. From a spiritual or metaphysical viewpoint, which is associated with oneness, there are infinite possibilities - there is abundance. In the physical world, which is associated with dualism, there can only be limitation. Without limitation, there would be no material world! Everything that we can experience from the physical world is limited by time and space; otherwise it would not exist. Think about a glass of wine - without the glass you can't drink wine. The wine in this example represents the divine experience, and the glass represents the physical world. If you contemplate about this example, you arrive at the point where you see, that the physical world is only a vessel and not a destination.

Fear leads to insane thinking and insane loveless behavior. The binning of all conflicts and wars!

It's like a movie you watch. You identify with it, you disappear, and it elicits feeling. Often even strong emotions - people laugh and cry. It's the purpose of the movie to do this! However, the moment your attention goes to the edges of the screen, or when the film ends, you know it was a movie – not reality. It's a fascinating fact because for the mind it does not matter if it is real or not.

Think about an event in the past. Close your eyes for a moment and remember a situation that left a big impression on your life - something with a substantial emotional impact. Use your attention and dive into this event. Explore, and expand on it until it becomes genuine - again.

In this example, you brought back old memories into the present moment. But wha about a story or a situation that never happened?

Again, close your eyes for a moment and bring your attention inside a spaceship. Yo are strapped into a seat, and the spacecraft takes off. A few moments pass, and you fal asleep. When you wake up, you are standing in a vast valley. You look up in the sky, an you see something you never saw before. You are finding yourself in a state of absolut bliss. It's the most beautiful thing that you have ever experienced. It takes your breatl away. You have completely emerged in it.

Now open your eyes, and you will notice that you had an experience, you had feelings This spaceship situation never happened to you, it was all imagined, but it seemed a real as the previous experience, right?

For your mind it makes no difference if you experience something you perceive as real, you remember an event from the past, or you imagine something.

It's the reason why the experience of fear seems real to you. The moment you step back and you free your attention, the fear disappears. The same as recognizing the edges of a movie.

Behavioral research experiments show that we invest more energy to move away from an unpleasant situation, then towards reaching a goal. You can observe this at demon- strations and political campaigns, which are mostly against something, rather than for something.

Sadly, fear is the primary motivation of most people.

Fear moves us away from something unpleasant that has either happened in the past, is happening right now, or may occur in the future. It's the pure drive away from discom- fort. It is therefore rarely a conscious decision. It's instead a reaction to a situation or stimuli we no longer want to experience. It acts like a hardwired biological trigger - no awareness is present. That's why every fear-driven motivation will usually lead to an uncontrolled, more or less random outcome.

Your mind operates through separation - it is based on a dualistic concept. The mind can only dissect, analyze, take apart, strip down or take into pieces. It is perfect that way and therefore a fantastic tool. That's why it is challenging for the mind to make a decision based on love.

Shifting from Fear to Love

When you experience fear, expand your attention. Take a look around, notice something you haven't seen before. At this moment you are becoming aware of the present, and you now can choose if you either proceed or not proceed with any fear-based action. This process takes time and needs to be practiced daily.

Remember, when you act on fear you are choosing limitations and restrictions.

This is where faith comes in. Faith is visionary, and it's allowing a higher power to come forward. An intentional force to move in. This higher power is beyond the mind. Faith is the remembering that there is a perfect solution, which is in alignment with nature. A solution, that in the interest of all parties, of everything that is affected by it. You don't know it but it's there.

It's like on a foggy day when you drive home. You see only 100 feet, but you know the street is there, the signs are there, and eventually when you follow them it will bring you home.

The moment you make this shift from fear to love you will recognize it as a warm feeling in your heart. A sense of expanding and inclusion, rather than contraction and separation.

Gerald G. Jampolsky brings this to the point by saying 'Love is letting go of fear.'

Fear related decisions are usually based on a thought loop. You start with the idea that you need money to survive. It's what the current economic model teaches us from the early beginning of our life. This 'belief,' which is based on limitation and scarcity, cause all further decisions, which then leads to more limitations and deficiency.

A limitation is the only outcome of the creation of the mind. It's the process of an idea that has been manifested into physical reality. Again, all material manifestations are limited; otherwise they cannot exist in time and space.

Money in its original context is a form of exchange between goods and services. Products and services have to come first, and then they can be exchanged for money. Money is used for the transfer of goods and services from one hand into another hand. It simplifies the transaction. Without money you need to trade a pig with a carpet, a hen with vegetable and so on – very impractical.

Trading without money would be impossible in our current economic structure with almost 8 billion people and trillions of transactions per day.

By the way - only banks can 'make' money. The rest of us have to take it from someone else! Saying you have to make money is a false assumption that has spread the world like a virus.

Any decision, which is based on 'making money' means you are setting yourself up to experience scarcity.

Every decision that is based on love is in complete alignment and harmony with everything else and therefore is not even a choice. It's the alignment, the natural flow of the unfolding process of life itself. Every decision on fear is the separation from life and eventually causes us and others harm and suffering.

The Ego - Money Connection

„The greatest conflicts are not between two people but between one person and himself." - Garth Brooks, American singer and songwriter

In a very simplified way, you could say that we humans live in two worlds at the same time. There is the metaphysical or spiritual world, and there is the physical world. The fact is, we are the source of the metaphysical or spiritual word, and what we experience as the physical world is nothing else than a grant illusion, which is created and orchestrated by our mind. This may sound very strange to you – especially the illusionary part.

In our usual day by day experience, we perceive the physical world as real, and as the source of our experience. However, from time to time we also have spiritual experiences, and we question ourselves to what extent we have free will. When we make decisions based on worldly experiences we adapt and react, we do not create. When we base our decisions on the metaphysical world, the source of who we are, we decide and create.

Because of the separations of this apparent two worlds we are often confused. We are surprised by the outcome when we use the rules of the physical world and apply them to the spiritual world – and the other way around.

It's the human dilemma, and it only can be managed by understanding the rules of the metaphysical world and the physical world together. In the western world, we are very well educated on the laws of the physical world. However, we are missing most of the education for the metaphysical world.

When we focus too much on the spiritual world, we neglect the physical world and th other way around. Too much focus on one of these world brings us out of balance. It i the equilibrium, and the proper use of these laws that make life a success. It is the wis dom to know who we are, that makes the experience in the physical world a pleasure without suffering.

Your real power comes from beyond this physical world.

In both worlds, we deal with illusions. All illusions are based on false assumptions. The ego is the illusion in the spiritual world and money is the illusion in the physical world.

What is the Ego?

The ego is a sum of beliefs and identities that we have collected over a lifetime, a per sonality created by pros and cons, likes and dislikes and endless opinions.

These beliefs that form an identity (sometimes more than one) are an attempt to keep us functioning inside a social and political structure. It's a pursuit to align a person with a higher hierarchy. The more top hierarchy's primary intention is control over you. Thinking and acting from this state of mind can only serve the more upper au thority - e.g., the economy, the government or the banks. You are operating as a slave and you don't even know it.

Without any conditioned beliefs, concepts and identities you are a free person that only serves the higher purpose of evolution. This is the state of sovereignty.

The ego is nothing else than an artificially created entity with the purpose to serve an artificial and limited hierarchy. The ego is not necessary for your life to flourish, it is hindering you to connect with the universal laws of abundance. The primary force of who you are.

In the physical world, we have created money. Money is a human invention, whose purpose is to simplify the transaction between different goods or services. It is a meaurement of value like a clock is a measurement of time, and inches are a measurement of length.

We add value in the form of a number to a product or service to make it more practical, because it simplifies the trade and exchange with other products or services.

Money also acts as a temporary store of value; however value itself is an artificial attribute. It has nothing to do with the product or service itself. How much value has a cat, a dog, a forest, an ocean, a tree, a person?

Adding value to a product or service creates artificial scarcity. It limits the value of the product or service. Whatever product or service you put a price sticker on, you create limitation. In some way it makes the service or product to compete with all the other goods and services. Therefore, it is an illusion and leads to a limited experience, which does not allow the nature of abundance to flow. The monetary system only serves a higher hierarchy. It serves the people that created it.

In reality, we don't need money at all. Abundance and wealth are created by human intelligence and sustainable resources with the intention to improve the quality of life.

Money does not create wealth!

Imagine, you have one million dollars in a bank safe. It will not create a new house, it will not produce food, and it will not improve your health. It's people, resources and creativity that can create wealth. What would happen when you and fifty other people get stranded on a deserted island. What would you do with your money? Open a bank?

Chapter V - A Blink Into the Future

Digital Money - A Solution?

"I think that the Internet is going to be one of the major forces for reducing the role of government. The one thing that's missing, but that will soon be developed, is a reliable e-cash..." - Milton Friedman, American economist

Without going too much into details, there is now a variety of digital money available. As of 2018, CoinMarketCap lists 1737 crypto-currencies.[75] The most common of them is Bitcoin. Thorsten Hoffmann explains in his movie documentary: 'The End of Money as we Know it' the story of Bitcoin.

Bitcoin is a system based on mathematical truths. Bitcoin is digital currency and computer software. Bitcoin is the shared code that creates a global payment network, using computers connected to the Internet. Bitcoins are a virtual currency, digital money created, stored and exchanged on that network.

But unlike virtual dollars created by a banker, this new currency was created with math by an unknown inventor. Bitcoin is an open-source software protocol, like the code that supports the Internet and email. Open-source means anyone, and everyone can use the protocol. No one person or company can control it. Every change to the software is public, open and transparent.

Bitcoin at its core is a cryptographic protocol, which is why it is also referred to as a 'crypto-currency.' The protocol creates unique pieces of digital property that can be transferred from one person to another. This protocol also makes it impossible to double-spend a Bitcoin, meaning you can't spend the same Bitcoin twice.

Bitcoins are generated by using an open-source computer program to solve complex math problems in a process known as mining. Each Bitcoin is defined by a public address and a private key, which are long strings of numbers and letters that give each a specific identity. This means that Bitcoin is not only a token of value but also a method for transferring that value.

In addition to having a unique digital fingerprint, Bitcoins are also characterized by their position in a public ledger of all Bitcoin transactions known as the blockchain. Buying a Bitcoin can be thought of as buying a spot in the blockchain, which then records your purchase publicly and permanently. [76]

The Blockchain Foundation

The blockchain is maintained by a distributed network of computers around the world. This decentralization means no one entity, such as a government, controls it. Transactions happen digitally from person to person, without middlemen such as banks or clearinghouses.

Blockchain refers to a technology that serves as a means of structuring and storing data. As such it is the ultimate foundation of the revolutionary crypto-currencies such as Bitcoin and Ether. The real breakthrough in coding capability permits participants to share digital ledgers back and forth over a computer network. Its genius and appeal lie in the fact that it does not require a central authority to run or oversee it. Since there is no meddling central authority like a central bank or boss to the system, no one party can interfere with the financial records.

In other words, the straight math makes sure that all the parties who participate are honest with each other. The blockchain is made up of concatenated transactions blocks. Nowadays, the technology has become so important and offers so many future possibilities for real-world applications, that over forty of the world's most important financial firms are experimenting with uses for it. [77]

Blockchains are also public record ledgers of all transactions in a crypto-currency which have ever taken place. For this reason, the chain is always expanding as every new record adds additional completed blocks to it. These become a part of the blockchain via a chronological and linear fashioned order. Every participating node receives a copy of this blockchain as it is updated. Nodes are computers which share a Bitcoin network connection that utilizes the system to validate and relay such transactions which were performed in it. The chain comes as an auto download once a computer network joins up to the Bitcoin network. This chain maintains full information on all balances and appropriate addresses from the very first transaction ever, all the way to the latest one which has been performed utilizing the block.

In the end, it is this blockchain that represents the primary technological advance offered by Bitcoin. It amounts to the proof and record of every transaction performed using the network. The blocks represent the current record in the chain that will ultimately record all or at least some of the recent transaction. After it is finished, this block will join the chain as part and parcel of the current and permanent database. Once a block is spoken for, a new block will become generated. Myriads of such blocks exist in the chain. They are linked one to another, much like a physical chain, in their correct chronological and linear order. Each block contains the hash of the previous block in it. A hash function is a mathematical process that takes input data of any size, performs an operation on it, and returns output data of a fixed size.[78]

It is always helpful to consider a real-world example to understand a somewhat complex concept like this one better. Traditional banking is a solid analogy. This blockchain is much like a complete history of banking records and transactions. Bitcoin transactions must be chronologically entered in the blockchain as real-world banking transactions are at financial institutions. Such blocks are something like the statements recording individual bank accounts and banking transactions.

The public Bitcoin network is the official record for all of these transactions. With this digital money, it is possible to be able to send and get money anywhere in the world at any given time. You don't have to worry about crossing borders, rescheduling for bank holidays or any other limitations one might think will occur when transferring money. You are in control of your money with Bitcoin. Again, there is no central authority figure in the Bitcoin network.

Merchants cannot charge extra fees on anything without being noticed. They must tall with the consumer before adding any charges. Payments in Bitcoin can be made and finalized without one's personal information being tied to the transactions. Because personal information is kept hidden from prying eyes, Bitcoin protects against identity theft.

With the blockchain, all finalized transactions are available for everyone to see. However, the personal information is hidden. The Bitcoin protocol cannot be manipulated by any person, organization, or government.

The Bitcoin network replaces banks and bankers. Digital currency cannot be debased with cheap metals or printed by the billion at will.

This new digital currency can be purchased online with a credit card or in person with cash. And it has the five key characteristics of money. But is it a store of value? Is it stable or will it diminish over time, like a commodity rendered useless, or a crop that fails? The ultimate power of a cryptocurrency is unleashed by mainstream adoption and an ever-growing volume of transactions.

Currently 69% of the population (2.3 billion) have no bank account.[79] With Bitcoin, a mobile phone with an Internet connection is now a bank, with access to the global marketplace. What happens when Bitcoin services and infrastructure and Bitcoin wallets and payment processors start going into these countries. These people will be able to gain benefits from trade where they could not previously. They will be able to send home money, international remittance, which is one of the major pain points of the current financial system.

You do not need a bank account. You need an Internet connection and a wallet to get et up. It's a tool to give people access into the global ecosystem and give them a prom- se for an economic future. Accurately provide a way for them not to be dependent on a government, that could shut down their bank accounts, or even could go into their bank accounts and take out finances.

However, there are also disadvantages. The price or value of a bitcoin fluctuates like any other currency. As more businesses, media, and trading centers begin to accept Bitcoin, its' price will eventually settle down. If you lose your passwords, or are fooled into pay- ing the wrong person, you can never get your money back. It is like digital cash. For a seller, this means no chargeback risks.

The total number of bitcoins will be capped when it reaches 21 million. Each bitcoin will be worth more and more as the total number of Bitcoins maxes out. It, therefore, may reward early adopters. Since each bitcoin will be valued higher with each passing day, the question of when to spend becomes important.

A cryptocurrency that can only be created and transferred by computer networks may be the next step of the digital revolution. The digital age has fundamentally changed the world. We have embraced digitized music, film, medical records, communications, the Internet.

The free exchange of information and currency can fuel revolutions, help in a disaster. But our money is shackled to the 20th century, manipulated by governments and banks.

Imagine payments without a middleman, investments without a broker, loans without a bank, and insurance without an underwriter. Charities without a trustee, Escrow without an agent, betting without a bookie, and record keeping without an accoun- tant.

Universal Basic Income

„Basic Income is not a utopia, it's a practical business plan for the next step of the human journey" - Jeremy Rifkin, American economic and social theorist, writer, public speaker

Universal basic income (UBI) is a model for providing all citizens of a country or other geographic area with a given sum of money, regardless of their income, resources or employment status. The purpose of the UBI is to prevent or reduce poverty and increase equality among citizens.

In the most common UBI implementation, identical periodic payments are made to all individuals and the tax system ensures that funds are returned to the system from those with higher incomes. Usually, the amount is gauged for subsistence: enough to take care of the individual's basic needs, but not enough to provide a lot of frills.[80]

Recently, UBI has been in the news as one way proposed to support a workforce displaced by automation. Elon Musk, Mark Zuckerberg, and many others believe that robots and AI-enhanced software may replace most human labor in a not-too-distant future scenario sometimes called the robot economy.

Critics of guaranteed income argue that it would be too expensive to implement and would create a disincentive to work. Proponents, on the other hand, believe that it could be cheaper in the long run, considering the effects of poverty, and that, furthermore, it would promote creativity and entrepreneurship among those freed from the struggle to survive.

One striking thing about guaranteeing a basic income is that it's always had support both on the left and on the right – albeit for different reasons. Martin Luther King embraced the idea, but so did the right-wing economist Milton Friedman, while the Nixon Administration even tried to get a basic-income guarantee through Congress. These days, among younger thinkers on the left, the UBI is seen as a means of ending poverty, combatting rising inequality, and liberating workers from the burden of crappy jobs. For thinkers on the right, the UBI seems like a simpler, and more libertarian, alternative to the thicket of anti-poverty and social-welfare programs. [81]

There are signs that the UBI may be an idea whose time has come. Switzerland held a referendum on a basic income in 2018 (though it lost badly); Finland is going to run a UBI experiment next year; and Y-Combinator, a Silicon Valley incubator firm, is sponsoring a similar test in Oakland.

Why now?

In the United States, the new interest in the UBI is driven in part by anxiety about how automation will affect workers. Bhaskar Sunkara, the publisher of the socialist magazine Jacobin, said, "People are fearful of becoming redundant, and there's this sense that the economy can't be built to provide jobs for everyone." In the short run, concerns about robots taking all our jobs are probably overstated. But the appeal of a basic income – a kind of Social Security for everyone – is easy to understand. It's easy to administer; it avoids the paternalism of social-welfare programs that tell people what they can and cannot buy with the money they're given. Also, if it's truly universal, it could help destigmatize government assistance. As Sunkara puts it, "Universal programs build social solidarity, and they become politically easier to defend."

The UBI is often framed as a tool for fighting poverty, but it would have other substantial benefits. By providing an income cushion, it would increase workers' bargaining power, potentially driving up wages. It would make it easier for people to take risks with their job choices, and to invest in education. There were small-scale experiments in the United States during the 70s with basic-income guarantees, and they showed that young people with a basic income were more likely to stay in school; in New Jersey, kids' chances of graduating from high school increased by twenty-five percent.

The critics of the UBI argue that handing people cash, instead of targeted aid (like food stamps), means that much of the money will be wasted, and that a basic income will take away the incentive to work, lowering GDP and giving us a nation of lazy, demoralized people. But the example of the many direct-cash-grant programs in the developing world suggests that, as the Columbia economist Chris Blattman puts it, "the poor do not waste grants."

As for the work question, most of the basic-income experiments suggest that the disincentive effect wouldn't be significant; in Manitoba, working hours for men dropped by just one percent. It's certainly true that the UBI. would make it easier for people to think twice about taking unrewarding jobs. But that's a good consequence, not a bad one.

A basic income would not be cheap - depending on how the program was structured, it would likely cost at least twelve to thirteen percent of GDP. And, given the state of American politics, which renders the UBI. politically impossible for the time being. The most popular social-welfare programs in the U.S. all seemed utopian at first. Until the nineteen-twenties, no state in the union offered any kind of old-age pension; by 1935, we had Social Security.

Guaranteed health care for seniors was attacked as unworkable and socialist; now Medicare is uncontroversial. If the UBI comes to be seen as a kind of insurance against a radically changing job market, rather than simply as a handout, the politics around it will change. When this happens, it's easy to imagine a basic income going overnight from entirely improbable to necessary. [82]

A New Path - The Resource Based Economy

"What will drive people if they don't have money or reward? The reward is the end of war, the end of poverty, most crime, and the end of begging for medical care. Everyone will be cared for and educated. There will be no taxation, and no advantage group. No technical elitism, or any other kind of elitism. If that isn't incentive enough, then I don't know what is." - Jacque Fresco, American futurist and social engineer

Jacque Fresco originated the term and meaning of a Resource Based Economy. The following is a summary of „The Venus Project."

It's a holistic socio-economic system in which all goods and services are available without the use of money, credits, barter or any other system of debt or servitude. All resources become the common heritage of all of the inhabitants, not just a select few.

The premise upon which this system is based, is that the Earth is abundant with plentiful resource; our practice of rationing resources through monetary methods is irrelevant and counter-productive to our survival. [83]

Modern society has access to highly advanced technology and can make available food, clothing, housing and medical care; update our educational system; and develop a limitless supply of renewable, non-contaminating energy. By supplying an efficiently designed economy, everyone can enjoy a very high standard of living with all of the amenities of a high technological society.

A resource-based economy would utilize existing resources from the land and sea, phys ical equipment, industrial plants, etc. to enhance the lives of the total population. In a economy based on resources rather than money, we could efficiently produce all of th necessities of life and provide a high standard of living for all.

In a resource-based economy all of the world's resources are held as the common her itage of all of Earth's people, thus eventually outgrowing the need for the artificia boundaries that separate people.

This approach to global governance has nothing whatever in common with the presen aims of an elite to form a world government with themselves and large corporations a the helm, and the vast majority of the world's population subservient to them. Thi vision of globalization empowers each and every person on the planet to be the bes they can be, not to live in abject subjugation to a corporate governing body.

It would not only add to the well being of people, but they would also provide the nec essary information, that would enable them to participate in any area of their compe tence. The measure of success would be based on the fulfillment of one's pursuits rathe than the acquisition of wealth, property and power. [84]

At present, we have enough material resources to provide a very high standard of living for all of Earth's inhabitants. Only when the population exceeds the carrying capacity of the land do many problems such as greed, crime and violence emerge. By overcom ing scarcity, most of the crimes and even the prisons of today's society would no longer be necessary.

A resource-based economy would make it possible to use technology to overcome scarce resources by applying renewable sources of energy, computerizing and automat ing manufacturing and inventory. Designing safe energy-efficient cities and advanced transportation systems, providing universal health care, more relevant education. Most of all, generating a new incentive system, based on human and environmental concern.

Using Technology to our Advantage

„Humanity is acquiring all the right technology for all the wrong reasons." – R. Buckminster Fuller, American architect, systems theorist, author, designer, inventor and futurist

Many people believe that there is too much technology in the world today, and that technology is the primary cause of our environmental pollution. This is not the case. It is the abuse and misuse of technology that should be our primary concern. In a more humane civilization, instead of machines displacing people, they would shorten the workday, increase the availability of goods and services, and lengthen vacation time. If we utilize new technology to raise the standard of living for all people, then the infusion of machine technology would no longer be a threat. [85]

Are you aware that there are thousands of ingenious patents bought up by big corporations? They are locked up in safes because they are so powerful that they disrupt entire product lines and whole companies. We already have solutions to produce free energy for all people on the planet. Here are a few examples:

Free Energy

Nikola Tesla was more than just the inspiration for a hair metal band; he was also an undisputed genius. In 1899, he figured out a way to bypass fossil-fuel-burning power plants and power lines, proving that "free energy" could be harnessed using ionization in the upper atmosphere to produce electrical vibrations.

J.P. Morgan, who had been funding Tesla's research, had a bit of buyer's remorse when he realized that free energy for all wasn't as profitable as, say, actually charging people for every watt of energy use. J. P. Morgan then drove another nail in free energy's coffin by chasing away other investors, ensuring Tesla's dream would die. [86]

The American Streetcar

In 1921, the streetcar industry earned $1 billion, causing General Motors to bleed $65 million in the face of a thriving industry. GM retaliated by buying (or pressuring out of business) hundreds of independent railway companies, boosting the market for gas guzzling GM buses and cars. The face of American transportation was all cars, cars, cars for the next half-century - mass transportation died because of monetary focus. [87]

Long Lasting Energy Efficient Bulbs

Phillips, GE, and Osram engaged in a conspiracy from 1924 to 1939 with the goal of controlling the fledgling light-bulb industry, according to a report published in Time magazine six years later. The alleged cartel set prices and suppressed competing technologies that would have produced longer-lasting and more efficient light bulbs. [88]

By the time the plot dissolved, the industry-standard incandescent bulb was established as the dominant source of artificial light across Europe and North America. Not until the late 1990s did compact fluorescent bulbs begin to edge into the worldwide lighting market as an alternative. After that LED bulbs finally arrived in the market, which now uses only 10% of power compared to the old technology.

The Electric Car is Back

More than 20 years ago there was already a solution for cars that have an MPG of 99 miles! There are leggings that never tear, and matches that light up again and again. Products can be manufactured that last forever, but would kill an industry that lives from these products that break down!

Tesla, a private company, is finally bold enough to interrupt the oil-fueled car industry by making electric cars for the masses. They even establish already a countrywide net of

harging stations. By the end of 2017, they had over 400.000 orders for a car that peo-
le may get in 1-2 years. Have you ever heard anything that comes close to that from a
asoline-powered vehicle?

ocus on Resource-Based Energy

acque Fresco and the Venus project are convinced that a resource-based world econo-
ny would also involve all-out efforts to develop new, clean, and renewable sources of
nergy: geothermal; controlled fusion; solar; photovoltaic; wind, wave, and tidal pow-
r; and even fuel from the oceans. We would eventually be able to have energy in un-
imited quantity that could propel civilization for thousands of years. [89]

A resource-based economy must also be committed to the redesign of our cities, trans-
ortation systems, and industrial plants, allowing them to be energy efficient, clean,
nd conveniently serve the needs of all people.

What else would a resource-based economy mean? Technology intelligently and effi-
iently applied, conserves energy, reduces waste, and provides more leisure time. With
utomated inventory on a global scale, we can maintain a balance between production
nd distribution. Only nutritious and healthy food would be available and planned
bsolescence would be unnecessary and non-existent in a resource-based economy.

As we outgrow the need for professions based on the monetary system, for instance,
awyers, bankers, insurance agents, marketing and advertising personnel, salespersons,
nd stockbrokers, a considerable amount of wasted creativity will be eliminated.

Considerable amounts of energy would also be saved by eliminating the duplication of
competitive products such as tools, eating utensils, pots, pans and vacuum cleaners. A
choice is good, but instead of hundreds of different manufacturing plants and all the
paperwork and personnel required to turn out similar products, only a few of the highest quality would be needed to serve the entire population.

Our only shortage is the lack of creative thought and intelligence in ourselves and our elected leaders to solve these problems. The most valuable, untapped resource today is human ingenuity.

The Elimination of Debt

With the elimination of debt says Jacque Fresco, the fear of losing one's job will no longer be a threat. This assurance, combined with education on how to relate to one another in a much more meaningful way, could considerably reduce both mental and physical stress and leave us free to explore and develop our abilities.

If the thought of eliminating money troubles you, consider the island example again: If a group of people with gold, diamonds, and money were stranded on an island that had no resources such as food, clean air, and water, their wealth would be irrelevant to their survival. It is only when resources are scarce that money can be used to control their distribution. One could not, for example, sell the air we breathe or water abundantly flowing down from a mountain stream. Although air and water are valuable, in abundance they cannot be sold.

Money is only significant in a society when specific resources for survival must be rationed, and the people accept money as an exchange medium for the scarce resources. Money is a social convention, an agreement if you will. It is neither a natural resource nor does it represent one. It is not necessary for survival, unless we have been conditioned to accept it as such.

We usually don't pay for air and tap water, because it is in such high abundance, selling it would be pointless. So then, logically speaking, if resources and technologies applicable to creating everything in our societies such as houses, cities, and transportation were in high enough abundance, there would be no reason to sell anything. Likewise, if automation and machinery were so technologically advanced, as to relieve human beings of labor there would be no reason to have a job. And with these social aspects taking care of, there would be no reason to have money at all.

Focus on People Instead of Economy

The significant difference between a resource based economy and a monetary system is that a resource based economy is concerned with people and their well-being, where the financial system has become so distorted that the concerns of the people are secondary if they're there at all. Products are turned out for how much money you can get. If there is a problem in society and you can't earn money from solving it, then most likely it won't be done.

The resource-based economy is not close to anything that's been tried. And with all our technology today we can create abundance. It could be used to improve everyone's life-style. Abundance all over the world if we use our technology wisely and maintain the environment.

Solar energy has such abundance that one hour of light at high noon contains more power than what the entire world consumes in a year. If we could capture one-hundredth of a percent (.01%) of this energy the world would never have to use oil, gas or anything else. Solar energy is now the cheapest to produce!

The question is not availability, but the technology to harness it, and there are many advanced mediums today which could accomplish just that. If they were not hindered by the need to compete for market share with the established energy power structures.

Then there's wind energy. Wind energy has long been denounced as weak, and due to being location driven, impractical. This is not true. The US Department of energy admitted in 2007 that if the wind were fully harvested in just three of Americas 50 states, it could power the entire nation. And there are the unknown mediums of tidal and wave power.

Geothermal energy utilizes, what is called ,heat mining, which, through a simple process using water, can generate massive amounts of clean energy. In 2006 an MIT report on geothermal energy found that 13.000 Zetta Joule of power is currently available in the earth with the possibility of 2.000 Zetta Joule being easily tap-able wit improved technology.

The total energy consumption of all the countries on the planet is about half of a Zett Joule a Year. This means about 4000 years of planetary power could be harnessed i this medium alone. And when we understand that the earth's heat generation is con stantly renewed, this energy is limitless.

It could be used forever! These energy sources are only a few of the clean, renewabl mediums available. And as time goes on, we will find more. The grand realization i that we have total energy abundance without the need for pollution, traditional con servation, or in fact a price tag!

There is absolutely no reason, other than pure corrupt profit interest that every singl vehicle in the world cannot be electric and utterly clean with zero need for gasolin Besides that, we can finally go back to the idea of building public transportation that i many times more efficient, faster and fun.

By the way, this may already be happening soon. As mentioned before, Elon Musk ha introduced the idea of building Hyper Loops. A fantastic way to connect big citie with a new transportation system that is relative cheap to build, uses less energy tha airplanes, and could even reach faster speed than planes. It would not only reduce trav el time and resources, but it would also reduce the stress and complexity of today' check-in and checkout procedures on airports.

Afterword

We are currently living in a time with one of the most fundamental changes we have ever faced on this planet. Many people believe that our modern civilization caused this massive change, and therefore we are also responsible for it. That may be part of the story, but my conclusion tells me that there is more to it. That there is an intelligent driving force behind creation (maybe life itself), which is beyond our current understanding. Its destiny is the creation of an enlightened planetary civilization. The time to get there is not relevant!

On top of our western civilization stands the belief, that we are separate from each other and the environment, that we are just bodies that have no purpose, besides our survival. This belief is the framework of our western civilization, and it determines all other theories and concepts by which we live. It is a rational and bizarre concept and discards the natural principles of life. In the coming years, we hopefully understand, that this foolish concept brought us closer to our extinction.

Indigenous people, like the groups that live in the Amazon rainforest, or the native Indians see our species behave insanely. Who in their right mind would destroy its habitat from where they get nourished and fed? Who in their right mind would stash millions of products and not be upset when millions of other people starve to death. All this because we worship money over people and nature!

Money is an invention and was created for the purpose to exchange good and services. It got abused, corrupted and finally declared as the most valuable asset. It has even dethroned God.

It has become the dominant, thriving force on this planet, works now against us and threatens our survival. It creates scarcity instead of abundance. We have outgrown our current story of money and need to re-invent it as a first step toward adopting a new way of thinking. If the majority of people think that they need inches to build a house than clearly, we have gotten mad.

However, in the middle of this crisis, we see a new light emerging, which already points to a new concept on how we will start living the next decades, maybe centuries. Cryptocurrencies outside of the control of central banks and governments may lead in the right direction. The day will come we make smart decisions with our smartphones, instead of playing silly games to kill time. The time will come we realize that owning all means losing all.

The forgotten ancient truth, that we are all connected with each other and the environment, will be reborn and will lead to more responsibility. It will create much less competition and more cooperation and harmony. We will integrate - again - spiritual laws into our lives, and by that, more and more people will change their outlook and habits on how they operate their lives. The pressure on the old system will become so intense that it will slowly implode. Hopefully, this time, we will need no war to destroy the old system. It may slowly fall apart like a rotten shed, and from its soil, a new foundation will arise.

The question of "Why is God allowing this all?" will soon be laughable and replaced by a new understanding that God has nothing to do with it. It's our arrogant, hallucinating thinking that creates the opposite of what evolution and God have always intended - harmony, abundance, and peace.

As an old saying goes: „The mind divides, and the heart unites."

No longer can we rely on the top to bottom hierarchy that has governed civilizations for thousands of years. By 2017 we have grown to 7.6 billion people, and in not even a decade, the entire planet will be interconnected. We have started to build the most intelligent network on earth, the Internet. In the future, we will use it to create abundance worldwide. Borders will vanish because we will eventually understand that keeping the majority of the people poor comes at a high price.

We are very close to the point, where corporations could produce products at hardly any cost at all. Service will have a comeback because we have the urge for human connection. It's the human connection that makes us feel good, inspire us to think beyond ourselves, and let us thrive to be our best.

I hope that this book has given you an insight into our current monetary structure and also served as a source of inspiration that there is the groundwork for a better future.

Each of us is now the cornerstone of civilization, and each of us has to step up to its full potential. We slowly wake up and become adults. When you stop blaming others, you have the change to be responsible. When you are responsible, you will think differently and your action will make a difference. It may not be comfortable in the beginning, but rest assured your reward will be beyond your wildest dreams.

Please share the ideas of this book with your friends and colleagues. Feel free to share single paragraphs of this book online without my permission. Just quote my name and add a link to moneydeception.com or the book listing on amazon.com.

Free Ebook - The 100 Most Popular Financial Terms Explained

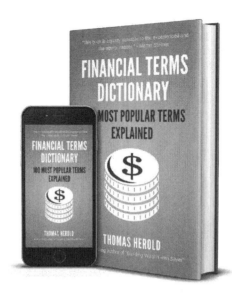

Need to lookup a financial term? Get the free Kindle version of the Financial Dictionary, which covers over 100 most popular and important financial terms - explained in detail and with examples. The 2018 edition also contains crypto-currencies terms like blockchain and Bitcoin.

Lookup & Learn Financial Terms

The author of this book created one of the most comprehensive financial dictionaries on the Internet. With over 1000 entries it covers the most important and frequently used financial terms. All terms are explained in clear and concise article style with practical examples.

Financial Dictionary Online

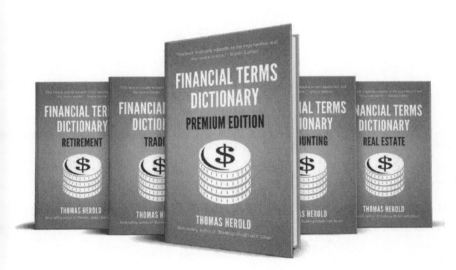

This entire financial dictionary is also available in Kindle or Paperback version and covers all major financial areas with 11 separate issues. Just go to amazon.com and search for ‚Thomas Herold‘ or use the amazon link below.

Look up the financial dictionary series
amazon.com/financial-terms-dictionary-series

Resources

Recommended Books and Documentaries

Investing
- Guide to Investing In Gold and Silver -*Michael Maloney*
- Bank On Yourself: The Life-Changing Secret to Protecting Your Financial Future - *Pamela Yellen*

Mindset
- Rich Dad's Prophecy - *Robert T. Kiyosaki, Sharon L. Lechterr*
- Global Shift: How A New Worldview Is Transforming Humanity - *Edmund J. Bourne*
- Life Inc.: How the World Became a Corporation and How to Take It Back - *Douglas Rushkoff*

Wealth
- Sustainable Wealth - *Axel Merk, William Poole*
- Unlimited Wealth: The Theory and Practice of Economic Alchemy - *Pilzer, Paul Zane*
- The Wealthy Code; What the Wealthy Know About Money That Most People Will Never Know! - *George Antone*

Money & Currency
- The Creature from Jekyll Island: A Second Look at the Federal Reserve - *G. Edward Griffin, Dan Smoot*
- This Time is Different: Eight Centuries of Financial Folly - *Carmen M. Reinhart, Kenneth Rogoff*
- The End of Money and the Future of Civilization - *Thomas H. Greco Jr.*
- End the Fed - *Ron Paul*

Money as Debt
- Empire of Debt: The Rise of an Epic Financial Crisis - *William Bonner, Addison Wiggin*

Web of Debt: The Shocking Truth About Our Money System and How We Can Break Free - *Ellen Hodgson Brown*
Debt: The First 5,000 Years - *David Graeber*

Economy & Society
The Third Industrial Revolution: How Lateral Power Is Transforming Energy, the Economy, and the World - *Jeremy Rifkin*
The Way We're Working Isn't Working: The Four Forgotten Needs That Energize Great Performance - *Tony Schwartz*
The Zero Marginal Cost Society: The Internet of Things, the Collaborative Commons, and the Eclipse of Capitalism - *Rifkin, Jeremy*
Getting a Grip: Clarity, Creativity, and Courage in a World Gone Mad - *Frances Moore Lappe*
Life Inc.: How the World Became a Corporation and How to Take It Back - *Douglas Rushkoff*

Beyond Money
The Best That Money Can't Buy: Beyond Politics, Poverty, & War - *Jacque Fresco*
Future by Design - *Jacques Fresco*
The Economics of Happiness - *Mark Anielski*
Grunch of Giants - *R. Buckminster Fuller*
Treknonomics – The Economics of Star Trek - *Manu Saadi*
Anthology for the New Millennium - *Thomas T. K. Zung, Buckminster Fuller*

Scarcity Versus Abundance
Abundance: The Future Is Better Than You Think - *Peter H. Diamandis, Steven Kotler*
The Soul of Money: Reclaiming the Wealth of Our Inner Resources - *Lynne Twist, Teresa Barker*
Sacred Economics: Money, Gift, and Society in the Age of Transition - *Eisenstein, Charles*

Documentary Films
Money as Debt - *Paul Grignon*
Money Versus Currency – Hidden Secrets Of Money - *Mike Maloney*
Finance and Capital Markets - *Khan Academy*
Zeitgeist – Part III Moving Forward - *Peter Joseph*
Money and Life - *Katie Teague*
Heist – Who Stole The American Dream? - *Donald Goldmacher*

Science & Spirit
Spontaneous Evolution - *Bruce Lipton*
The Biology of Belief - *Bruce Lipton*

Metaphysics & Psychology
A Return to Love - *Marianne Williamson*

- The Law of Devine Compensation - *Marianne Williamson*
- How to Know God - D*eepak Chopra*
- Conversations with God - *Neale Donald Walsh*
- Mind Before Matter: Vision of a New Science of Consciousness - *Trish Pfeiffer*
- The Passion Test: The Effortless Path to Discovering Your Destiny - *Janet Attwood*
- Mind Programming: From Persuasion and Brainwashing, to Self-Help and Practical Meta physics - *Eldon Taylor*

Spirituality
- A New Earth: Awakening to Your Life's Purpose - *Eckhart Tolle*

Philosophie & Science
- The Chaos Point: The World at the Crossroads - *Ervin Laszlo*
- Quantum Shift in the Global Brain - *Ervin Laszlo*
- The Immortal Mind: Science and the Continuity of Consciousness beyond the Brain - *Ervin Laszlo*

Bibliography

[1] Peter Joseph - Zeitgeist: Moving Forward. Retrieved from http://www.zeitgeistmovie.com/

[2] Oxfam - Reward Work not Wealth https://www.oxfam.org/en/research/reward-work-not-wealth

[3] Gary Gibson - The Daily Reckoning https://dailyreckoning.com/the-fall-of-the-roman-denarius/

[4] Positive Money - Consequences of the Current Money System http://positivemoney.org/issues/

[5] Positive Money - Why Are House Prices so High? http://positivemoney.org/issues/house-prices/

[6] Sacred Economics - Charles Eisenstein http://sacred-economics.com/

[7] Thrive Global - Drake Baer The Number Of Americans On Antidepressants Has Skyrocketed

[8] Forbes Business - Survey: 69% Of Americans Have Less Than $1,000 https://www.forbes.com/sites/niallmccarthy/2016/09/23/survey-69-of-americans-have-less-than-1000-in-savings-infographic/#dcfb5a41ae67

[9] Learning Markets - Understanding the Fractional Reserve Banking System https://www.learningmarkets.com/understanding-the-fractional-reserve-banking-system/

[10] Fox News - I tried to open a lemonade stand http://www.foxnews.com/opinion/2012/02/24/tried-to-open-lemonade-stand.html

[11] Chris Horlacher - The Decline and Fall of the Roman Denarius https://dollarvigilante.com/blog/2012/02/28/the-decline-and-fall-of-the-roman-denarius.html

[12] Wikipedia - Currency War https://en.wikipedia.org/wiki/Currency_war

[13] Duncan Cameron - Banks and the derivatives scam http://rabble.ca/columnists/2012/05/banks-and-derivatives-scam

[14] Duncan Cameron - Banks and the derivatives scam http://rabble.ca/columnists/2012/05/banks-and-derivatives-scam

[15] Simon Black - Sovereign Man https://www.sovereignman.com/trends/have-you-heard-of-this-digital-currency-thats-a-total-scam-18189/

[16] Simon Black - Sovereign Man https://www.sovereignman.com/trends/have-you-heard-of-this-digital-currency-thats-a-total-scam-18189/

[17] Sean Geddert - Seeking Alpha https://seekingalpha.com/article/4054626-part-1-silvers-price-manipulation

[18] Mike Turner - What is Missing from Education. Why are we not fixing it? http://www.miketurnerboise.com/why-dont-we-allow-students-to-learn-about-entrepreneurism/

19 Sameer Datye - Insurance: Selling Fear – Selling Hope! https://perspectives.tieto.com/blog/2017/06/insurance-selling-fear--selling-hope/

20 World Population Balance - Understanding Exponential Growth http://www.worldpopulationbalance.org/exponential-growth-tutorial/bacteria-exponential-growth.html

21 Alfie Kohn - The Case Against Competition http://www.alfiekohn.org/article/case-competition/

22 Wikipedia - Monopoly https://en.wikipedia.org/wiki/Monopoly

23 Markus Krajewski - The Great Lightbulb Conspiracy https://spectrum.ieee.org/tech-history/dawn-of-electronics/the-great-lightbulb-conspiracy

24 Christina H - 6 Secret Monopolies You Didn't Know Run the World http://www.cracked.com/article_18845_6-secret-monopolies-you-didnt-know-run-world.html

25 New America - Monopoly by the Numbers https://www.newamerica.org/open-markets/understanding-monopoly/monopoly-numbers/

26 John Burnett - Independent Farmers Feel Squeezed By Milk Cartel https://www.npr.org/templates/story/story.php?storyId=112002639

27 Wikipedia - Corporate welfare https://en.wikipedia.org/wiki/Corporate_welfare

28 Wellfare Info http://www.welfareinfo.org/corporate/

29 John White - How Corporate Welfare Is Killing Small Businesses https://www.inc.com/john-white/how-corporate-welfare-is-killing-small-businesses.html

30 John White - How Corporate Welfare Is Killing Small Businesses https://www.inc.com/john-white/how-corporate-welfare-is-killing-small-businesses.html

31 Sam Becker - The 8 Biggest Corporate Welfare Recipients in America https://www.cheatsheet.com/business/high-on-the-hog-the-top-8-corporate-welfare-recipients.html

32 Sam Becker - The 8 Biggest Corporate Welfare Recipients in America https://www.cheatsheet.com/business/high-on-the-hog-the-top-8-corporate-welfare-recipients.html

33 Steve Pavlina - 10 Reasons You Should Never Get a Job https://www.stevepavlina.com/blog/2006/07/10-reasons-you-should-never-get-a-job/

34 Dustin Mineau - The 401k is a Government Subsidy for Wall Street https://www.dailykos.com/stories/2012/9/17/1132891/-The-401k-is-a-Government-Subsidy-for-Wall-Street

35 Barry D. Moore - 39 Stock Market Statistics https://www.liberatedstocktrader.com/stock-market-statistics/

36 Dustin Mineau - The 401k is a Government Subsidy for Wall Street https://www.dailykos.com/stories/2012/9/17/1132891/-The-401k-is-a-Government-Subsidy-for-Wall-Street

[37] Bruce Lipton - Spontaneous Evolution https://www.brucelipton.com/resource/article/spontaneous-evolution-new-scientific-realities-are-bringing-spirit-back-matter

[38] Bruce Lipton - Spontaneous Evolution https://www.brucelipton.com/resource/article/spontaneous-evolution-new-scientific-realities-are-bringing-spirit-back-matter

[39] Jean Kilbourne - Can't Buy My Love https://www.amazon.com/Cant-Buy-My-Love-Advertising/dp/0684866005

[40] Joe Dubs - Propaganda: Mind Manipulation and Manufacturing Consent https://wakeup-world.com/2015/11/16/propaganda-mind-manipulation-and-manufacturing-consent/

[41] Tim Adams - How Freud got under our skin https://www.theguardian.com/education/2002/mar/10/medicalscience.highereducation

[42] Paul Roberts - Impulse Society https://theimpulsesociety.wordpress.com/books/about/

[43] Princeton University - Study: Brain battles itself over short-term rewards, long-term goals https://www.princeton.edu/pr/news/04/q4/1014-brain.htm

[44] Maia Szalavitz - The Secrets of Self-Control http://healthland.time.com/2011/09/06/the-secrets-of-self-control-the-marshmallow-test-40-years-later/

[45] Sofo Archon - The Weapon of Fear https://theunboundedspirit.com/the-weapon-of-fear-how-they-use-fear-to-manipulate-you/

[46] Greg Timble - Definition of Religion https://www.gregtrimble.com/meaning-of-the-word-religion/

[47] David G - How Fear is Used to Turn You Against Spirituality http://consciousreporter.com/conspiracy-against-consciousness/how-fear-is-used-to-turn-you-against-spirituality/

[48] David G - How Fear is Used to Turn You Against Spirituality http://consciousreporter.com/conspiracy-against-consciousness/how-fear-is-used-to-turn-you-against-spirituality/

[49] Jeremy Lent - The New Mind Manipulators https://www.huffingtonpost.com/jeremy-lent/the-new-mind-manipulators_b_9760268.html

[50] The Statistics Portal https://www.statista.com/statistics/264810/number-of-monthly-active-facebook-users-worldwide/

[51] Jeremy Lent - The New Mind Manipulators https://www.huffingtonpost.com/jeremy-lent/the-new-mind-manipulators_b_9760268.html

[52] Serge Kahili King - Personal Sovereignty https://www.huna.org/html/perssov.html

[53] Serge Kahili King - Personal Sovereignty https://www.huna.org/html/perssov.html

[54] Alan Watts - Does it Matter https://www.amazon.de/exec/obidos/ASIN/1577315855/braipick00-21

45 Alan Watts - Does it Matter https://www.amazon.de/exec/obidos/ASIN/1577315855/braipick00-21

46 Charles Eisenstein - Sacred Economics http://sacred-economics.com/

47 Charles Eisenstein - Sacred Economics http://sacred-economics.com/

48 Charles Eisenstein - Sacred Economics http://sacred-economics.com/sacred-economics-chapter-12-negative-inter-st-economics/

49 Charles Eisenstein - Negative-Interest Economics http://sacred-economics.com/

50 Wikipedia - Compound Interest https://en.wikipedia.org/wiki/Compound_interest

51 Robert Kiyosaki - Rich Dad Poor Dad https://en.wikipedia.org/wiki/Rich_Dad_Poor_Dad

52 Alan Watts - Life and Listening http://brentwehmeyer.com/is-there-more-to-life-than-just-living/

53 Anthony Covalciuc - 5 Reasons the Future of Software is Open Source https://blog.sourcefabric.org/en/news/blog/3592/5-Reasons-the-Future-of-Software-is-Open-Source.htm

54 Open Source Ecology - The mission of Open Source Ecology http://opensourceecology.org/about-overview/

55 Peter Diamondis - Abundance Insider http://www.diamandis.com/blog/abundance-insider-december-29-2017-edition

56 Wikipedia History of the Automobile https://en.wikipedia.org/wiki/History_of_the_automobile

57 Wikipedia - Hyperloop https://en.wikipedia.org/wiki/Hyperloop

58 United States Department of Transportation - https://www.rita.dot.gov/bts/sites/rita.dot.gov.bts/files/publications/highlights_of_the_2001_national_household_travel_survey/html/section_02.html

59 Bruce Lipton - How Our Thoughts Control Our DNA https://www.brucelipton.com/blog/how-our-thoughts-control-our-dna

70 Bruce Lipton - How Our Thoughts Control Our DNA https://www.brucelipton.com/blog/how-our-thoughts-control-our-dna

71 The Golden Rule - Sayings from the Religions http://www.onenessonline.com/golden.htm

72 Jeffrey Moses - Oneness: Great Principles Shared by All Religions - https://www.amazon.com/Oneness-Principles-Religions-Revised-Expanded/dp/0345457633

73 Tamara Rant - Quantum Oneness https://consciouslifenews.com/quantum-oneness-physics-proves-simultaneous-ly-everywhere/1181269

74 (2003, January 1). Science. Retrieved from http://www.starstuffs.com/physcon/science.html

[75] CoinMarketCap - Lost of all Crypto-Currencies https://coinmarketcap.com/all/views/all/

[76] Bitcoin Organisation - Frequently Asked Questions https://bitcoin.org/en/faq

[77] Thomas Herold - What is a Blockchain? https://www.financial-dictionary.info/terms/blockchain/

[78] Corin Faife - Bitcoin Hash Functions Explained https://www.coindesk.com/bitcoin-hash-functions-explained/

[79] The World Bank - The Global Findex database https://globalfindex.worldbank.org/

[80] Margaret Rouse - Universal Basic Income http://whatis.techtarget.com/definition/universal-basic-income-UBI

[81] Margaret Rouse - Universal Basic Income http://whatis.techtarget.com/definition/universal-basic-income-UBI

[82] Margaret Rouse - Universal Basic Income http://whatis.techtarget.com/definition/universal-basic-income-UBI

[83] Jacque Fresco - The Venus Project https://www.thevenusproject.com/resource-based-economy/

[84] Jacque Fresco - The Venus Project https://www.thevenusproject.com/resource-based-economy/

[85] Jacque Fresco - The Venus Project https://www.thevenusproject.com/resource-based-economy/

[86] Rich Bard - The 18 Most Suppressed Inventions Ever http://gawker.com/5784025/the-18-most-suppressed-inventions-ever

[87] Rich Bard - The 18 Most Suppressed Inventions Ever http://gawker.com/5784025/the-18-most-suppressed-inventions-ever

[88] James HSU - Greed Suppresses Inventions, Slows Down Progress of Society http://thirdmonk.net/knowledge/greed-suppresses-inventions.html

[89] Peter Joseph - Zeitgeist: Moving Forward. Retrieved from http://www.zeitgeistmovie.com/

Printed in Great Britain
by Amazon

36625460R00156